Taste of Home

5 INGREDIENT DINNERS

TASTE OF HOME BOOKS • RDA ENTHUSIAST BRANDS, LLC • MILWAUKEE, WI

P. 188

1610 N. 2nd St., Suite 102,
Milwaukee WI 53212-3906

Visit us at tasteofhome.com for other Taste of Home books and products.

ISBN: 978-1-62145-885-2

CHIEF CONTENT OFFICER, HOME & GARDEN: Jeanne Sidner
CONTENT DIRECTOR: Mark Hagen
ASSOCIATE CREATIVE DIRECTOR, EDITORIAL PRODUCTS: Raeann Thompson
ART DIRECTOR: Maggie Conners
SENIOR DESIGNER: Jazmin Delgado
DEPUTY EDITOR, COPY DESK: Dulcie Shoener
COPY EDITOR: Kara Dennison

COVER PHOTOGRAPHER: Mark Derse
SET STYLIST: Melissa Franco
FOOD STYLIST: Shannon Norris
PICTURED ON COVER:
Glazed Roast Chicken, p. 85

PICTURED ON TITLE PAGE:
Grilled Ribeye with Garlic Blue Cheese Mustard Sauce, p. 69

Printed in China
3 5 7 9 10 8 6 4 2

CONTENTS

P. 128

P. 18

P. 177

SHORT ON TIME?

Keep an eye out for these handy icons to help you quickly identify recipes that fit your schedule.

Fast Fix Dishes are table-ready in 30 minutes (or less!)—from the time you open the fridge to when you put the meal on the table!

Freeze Make-ahead dishes include instructions for freezing and reheating.

HOW WE COUNT TO FIVE

When counting the ingredients in our recipes, we exclude these essentials: Water, salt, pepper and oils. We also do not count optional ingredients such as garnishes.

MORE WAY TO CONNECT WITH US:

30-DAY MEAL PLANNER

CREATE MEMORABLE MENUS BY PAIRING ENTREES ALONGSIDE "SERVE IT WITH" SUGGESTIONS YOU CAN QUICKLY PICK UP AT THE GROCERY STORE.

Pressure-Cooker Tequila Salsa Chicken p. 16

SERVE IT WITH
- Corn tortillas
- Black beans

Ham & Cheese Potato Casserole, p. 23

SERVE IT WITH
- Biscuits
- Asparagus

Mexican Bubble Pizza, p. 31

SERVE IT WITH
- Green salad
- Refried beans

Grilled Asian Salmon Packets, p. 34

SERVE IT WITH
- White rice
- Egg rolls

Texas-Style Brisket, p. 44

SERVE IT WITH
- Cornbread
- Baked beans

Dinner Poppers, p. 100

SERVE IT WITH
- Spanish rice
- Corn

White Wine Garlic Chicken, p. 107

SERVE IT WITH
- Dinner rolls
- Red potatoes

Eggs & Chorizo Wraps, p. 245

SERVE IT WITH
- Orange wedges
- Hash browns

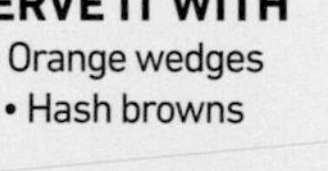

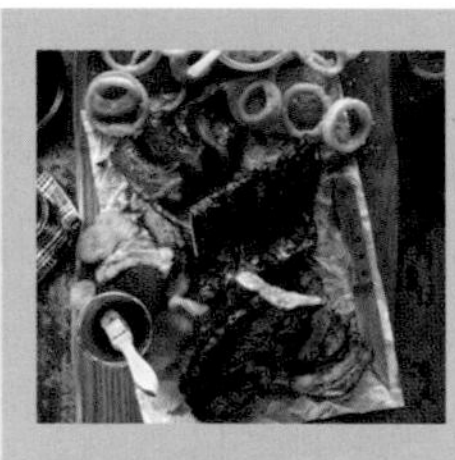

Habanero Raspberry Ribs, p. 118

SERVE IT WITH
- Mac and cheese
- Onion rings

Grilled Dijon Pork Roa p. 129

SERVE IT WITH
- Green salad
- Vegetable medley

Greek Spinach Bake, p. 182

SERVE IT WITH
- Fruit salad
- Muffins

Feta-Stuffed Portobello Mushrooms p. 186

SERVE IT WITH
- Buttered gnocchi
- French bread

Grilled Pimiento Cheese Sandwiches p. 195

SERVE IT WITH
- Tomato soup
- Potato chips

Hawaiian Pulled Pork Lettuce Wraps, p. 203

SERVE IT WITH
- Hawaiian dinner rolls
- Pineapple slices

Mediterranean Meatb Sandwiches, p. 216

SERVE IT WITH
- Pasta salad
- Carrot sticks

Brien Sausage Skillet, p. 250

SERVE IT WITH
• Toast
• Fruit salad

Fiesta Ravioli, p. 57

SERVE IT WITH
• Breadsticks
• Fruit salad

Smash Burgers, p. 65

SERVE IT WITH
• French fries
• Pickles

Glazed Spatchcocked Chicken, p. 88

SERVE IT WITH
• Stir-fried vegetables
• Baked potatoes

Romano Basil Turkey Breast, p. 95

SERVE IT WITH
• Stuffing
• Green beans

ewered Ginger Shrimp With Plums, p. 149

SERVE IT WITH
• Buttered noodles
• Whole wheat bread

Sage-Rubbed Salmon, p. 162

SERVE IT WITH
• Clam chowder
• Wild rice

Dad's Famous Stuffies, p. 167

SERVE IT WITH
• Pasta salad
• Tater Tots

Artichoke Cod with Sun-Dried Tomatoes p.169

SERVE IT WITH
• Couscous
• Watermelon slices

Bean & Cheese Quesadillas, p. 175

SERVE IT WITH
• Tortilla chips
• Spanish rice

weet & Tangy Pulled Pork, p. 219

SERVE IT WITH
• Sweet potato fries
• Pickles

Hash Brown Breakfast Casserole, p. 231

SERVE IT WITH
• Melon slices
• Bacon

Cranberry Glazed Pork Chops, p. 113

SERVE IT WITH
• Brussels sprouts
• Mashed potatoes

Cottage Cheese Pancakes, p. 245

SERVE IT WITH
• Breakfast sausages
• Fresh berries

Fast Philly Cheesesteak Pizza, p. 50

SERVE IT WITH
• Garlic bread
• Green salad

MEAL-IN-ONE DINNERS

COUSCOUS & SAUSAGE-STUFFED ACORN SQUASH
P. 10

1

2

3

4

5

ONE-DISH ENTREES THAT CALL FOR ONLY A HANDFUL OF INGREDIENTS? CHECK THESE OUT!

SAUSAGE POTATO SUPPER

One Saturday night, I cooked sausage with potatoes and zucchini—the ingredients I had on hand. This last-minute supper has been a hit with all six of us ever since.

—Nancy Russell, Englewood, CO

Takes: 25 min.
Makes: 2 servings

- 2 small red potatoes, cubed
- 1 Tbsp. butter
- 1 small zucchini, cut into ¼-in. slices
- ⅛ tsp. garlic salt
- ½ lb. smoked sausage, cut into ½-in. slices
- ⅛ to ¼ tsp. pepper
- Grated Parmesan cheese, optional

1. In a small saucepan, combine potatoes and enough water to cover; bring to a boil. Reduce heat; cook, uncovered, until tender, 15-20 minutes.
2. In a large skillet, heat butter over medium-high heat; saute zucchini with garlic salt until crisp-tender. Add the sausage; cook and stir until browned.
3. Drain potatoes; stir into zucchini mixture. Sprinkle with pepper and, if desired, cheese.

2 cups: 448 cal., 37g fat (17g sat. fat), 91mg chol., 1396mg sod., 12g carb. (5g sugars, 1g fiber), 18g pro.

TACO BISCUIT BAKE

Your whole gang will enjoy this fresh Mexican bake. It's a tasty new take on tacos.

—Sara Martin, Whitefish, MT

Prep: 20 min. • **Bake:** 25 min.
Makes: 8 servings

- 1 lb. lean ground beef (90% lean)
- ⅔ cup water
- 1 envelope taco seasoning
- 2 tubes (12 oz. each) refrigerated buttermilk biscuits
- 1 can (15 oz.) chili con carne
- 1 cup shredded reduced-fat cheddar cheese
- Optional: Salsa and sour cream

1. In a large skillet, cook beef over medium heat until no longer pink, breaking it into crumbles; drain. Stir in the water and taco seasoning. Bring to a boil; cook and stir for 2 minutes or until mixture is thickened.
2. Meanwhile, quarter biscuits; place in a greased 13x9-in. baking dish. Layer with beef mixture, chili and cheese.
3. Bake, uncovered, at 375° for 25-30 minutes or until cheese is melted and biscuits are golden brown. Serve with salsa and sour cream if desired.

1 serving: 481 cal., 23g fat (10g sat. fat), 64mg chol., 1487mg sod., 46g carb. (5g sugars, 1g fiber), 24g pro.

SAUSAGE POTATO
SUPPER

COUSCOUS & SAUSAGE-STUFFED ACORN SQUASH

With a tiny apartment, zero counter space and only two people to feed, hefty meals are out. This acorn squash with couscous is just the right size.
—Jessica Levinson, Nyack, NY

Takes: 25 min.
Makes: 2 servings

- 1 medium acorn squash (about 1½ lbs.)
- ¼ tsp. salt
- ¼ tsp. pepper
- 1 Tbsp. olive oil
- 1 medium onion, chopped
- 2 fully cooked spinach and feta chicken sausage links (3 oz. each), sliced
- ½ cup chicken stock
- ½ cup uncooked couscous
- Crumbled feta cheese, optional

1. Cut squash lengthwise in half; remove and discard seeds. Sprinkle squash with salt and pepper; place in a microwave-safe dish, cut side down. Microwave, covered, on high for 10-12 minutes or until tender.
2. Meanwhile, in a large skillet, heat the oil over medium heat. Add the onion; cook and stir until tender and lightly browned, 5-7 minutes. Add the sausage; cook and stir 2-3 minutes or until lightly browned.
3. Add stock; bring to a boil. Stir in couscous. Remove from heat; let stand, covered, 5 minutes or until stock is absorbed. Spoon over squash. If desired, top with feta cheese.

1 serving: 521 cal., 15g fat (4g sat. fat), 65mg chol., 979mg sod., 77g carb. (11g sugars, 8g fiber), 25g pro.sugars, 6g fiber), 29g pro.

COUSCOUS & SAUSAGE-STUFFED ACORN SQUASH

TEST KITCHEN TIP
Leftover rice makes an easy alternative to the couscous in this dish. Have extra stuffing after Thanksgiving? It also makes a great substitute for the couscous.

HONEY HOISIN CHICKEN & POTATOES

When I was young, Tutu (my grandma) cooked up this blend of Asian and American flavors. The potatoes are delicious drizzled with the pan juices.
—Janet Yee, Phoenix, AZ

Prep: 10 min. • **Bake:** 50 min.
Makes: 4 servings

- 4 medium Yukon Gold potatoes (about 1¾ lbs.), cut into 1-in. pieces
- 1 large onion, cut into 1-in. pieces
- ½ cup hoisin sauce
- 3 Tbsp. honey
- ½ tsp. salt, divided
- ½ tsp. pepper, divided
- 4 bone-in chicken thighs (about 1½ lbs.)

1. Preheat oven to 400°. Place the potatoes and onion in a greased 13x9-in. baking pan. In a small bowl, mix hoisin sauce, honey, ¼ tsp. salt and ¼ tsp. pepper; add to potato mixture and toss to coat.
2. Place chicken over vegetables; sprinkle with remaining salt and pepper. Roast 50-60 minutes or until the potatoes are tender and a thermometer inserted in the chicken reads 170°-175°, basting occasionally with pan juices.

Freeze option: Cool chicken mixture. Freeze in freezer containers. To use, partially thaw in refrigerator overnight. Heat through slowly in a covered skillet until a thermometer inserted in chicken reads 165°, stirring occasionally; add broth or water if necessary.

1 chicken thigh with 1 cup potato mixture and 3 Tbsp. sauce: 561 cal., 16g fat (4g sat. fat), 82mg chol., 910mg sod., 75g carb. (27g sugars, 6g fiber), 29g pro.

CRANBERRY PORK & SWEET POTATOES

CRANBERRY PORK & SWEET POTATOES

With tender pork chops straight from the slow cooker and sweet potatoes flavored with applesauce, cranberry sauce and brown sugar, this is a wonderful meal for the holiday season.

—Doris Branham, Kingston, TN

Prep: 10 min. • **Cook:** 6 hours
Makes: 6 servings

- 1⅔ cups sweetened applesauce (about 15 oz.)
- 3 lbs. sweet potatoes (about 3 large), peeled and cut into 1-in. slices
- ¾ tsp. salt, divided
- ¼ tsp. pepper, divided
- ¼ cup packed brown sugar
- 6 bone-in pork loin chops (6 oz. each)
- 1 can (14 oz.) whole-berry cranberry sauce

1. Place the applesauce in a 6-qt. slow cooker. Top with sweet potatoes; sprinkle with ¼ tsp. salt, ⅛ tsp. pepper and brown sugar.

2. Place the pork chops over the potatoes; sprinkle with remaining salt and pepper. Spoon cranberry sauce over pork. Cook, covered, on low 6-8 hours or until pork and sweet potatoes are tender.

1 serving: 649 cal., 14g fat (5g sat. fat), 83mg chol., 412mg sod., 101g carb. (58g sugars, 9g fiber), 31g pro.

BEEFY FRENCH ONION POTPIE

I came up with this dish knowing my husband loves French onion soup, which makes a perfect base for this hearty, beefy potpie.
—Sara Hutchens, Du Quoin, IL

Takes: 30 min.
Makes: 4 servings

- 1 lb. ground beef
- 1 small onion, chopped
- 1 can (10½ oz.) condensed French onion soup
- 1½ cups shredded part-skim mozzarella cheese
- 1 tube (12 oz.) refrigerated buttermilk biscuits

1. Preheat oven to 350°. In a large skillet, cook beef and onion over medium heat 6-8 minutes or until beef is no longer pink, breaking beef into crumbles; drain. Stir in soup; bring to a boil.
2. Transfer to an ungreased 9-in. deep-dish pie plate; sprinkle with cheese. Bake 5 minutes or until cheese is melted. Top with biscuits. Bake 15-20 minutes longer or until biscuits are golden brown.

1 serving: 553 cal., 23g fat (10g sat. fat), 98mg chol., 1550mg sod., 47g carb. (4g sugars, 1g fiber), 38g pro.

BEEFY FRENCH ONION POTPIE

AIR-FRYER CHICKEN PESTO STUFFED PEPPERS

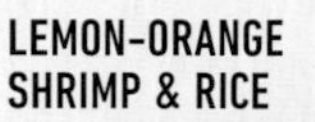

LEMON-ORANGE SHRIMP & RICE

AIR-FRYER CHICKEN PESTO STUFFED PEPPERS

On busy weeknights, I don't want to spend more than half an hour preparing dinner, nor do I want to wash a towering pile of dishes. This recipe delivers without having to sacrifice flavor!

—Olivia Cruz, Greenville, SC

Prep: 10 min. • **Cook:** 40 min.
Makes: 4 servings

- 4 medium sweet yellow or orange peppers
- 1½ cups shredded rotisserie chicken
- 1½ cups cooked brown rice
- 1 cup prepared pesto
- ½ cup shredded Havarti cheese
- Fresh basil leaves, optional

1. Preheat air fryer to 400°. Cut the peppers lengthwise in half; remove the stems and seeds. In batches, place the peppers in a single layer on tray in air-fryer basket. Cook until the skin starts to blister and the peppers are just tender, 10-15 minutes. Reduce air fryer temperature to 350°.
2. Meanwhile, in a large bowl, combine chicken, rice and pesto. When cool enough to handle, fill the peppers with the chicken mixture. In batches, cook until heated through, about 5 minutes. Sprinkle with the cheese; cook until cheese is melted, roughly 3-5 minutes. If desired, sprinkle with basil.

2 stuffed pepper halves: 521 cal., 31g fat (7g sat. fat), 62mg chol., 865mg sod., 33g carb. (7g sugars, 5g fiber), 25g pro.

LEMON-ORANGE SHRIMP & RICE

I enjoy Chinese takeout but not the calories. Here's an easy low-fat version that works with orange marmalade or peach or apricot preserves.

—Mary Wilhelm, Sparta, WI

Takes: 30 min.
Makes: 4 servings

- 2 pkg. (6.2 oz. each) fried rice mix
- 1½ lbs. uncooked medium shrimp, peeled and deveined
- 1 Tbsp. canola oil
- ¼ cup orange marmalade
- 2 tsp. grated lemon zest
- 3 cups frozen sugar snap peas, thawed

1. Prepare rice mix according to package directions, simmering for 10-15 minutes or just until rice is tender. Remove from pan.
2. In the same skillet, cook and stir shrimp in oil over medium-high heat for 4-6 minutes or until shrimp turn pink; stir in orange marmalade and lemon zest. Add the snap peas and fried rice; heat through, mixing gently to combine. Serve immediately.

1¾ cups: 631 cal., 14g fat (4g sat. fat), 222mg chol., 2009mg sod., 85g carb. (22g sugars, 5g fiber), 40g pro.

PRESSURE-COOKER
TEQUILA SALSA CHICKEN

PRESSURE-COOKER TEQUILA SALSA CHICKEN

I had this dish at a local Mexican restaurant when celebrating a friend's birthday. I fell in love with the spicy, smoky flavor from the tequila and decided to try it at home in my electric pressure cooker. It's also fabulous stuffed into flour tortillas.

—Trisha Kruse, Eagle, ID

Takes: 15 min. • **Makes:** 3 cups

- 1 envelope taco seasoning
- 1 lb. boneless skinless chicken breasts
- 1 cup chunky salsa
- ¼ cup tequila
- Hot cooked rice
- Optional: Avocado slices, chopped fresh cilantro and lime wedges

1. Sprinkle taco seasoning over chicken; place in a 6-qt. electric pressure cooker. Combine the salsa and tequila; pour over the chicken. Lock lid; close the pressure-release valve. Adjust to pressure-cook on high for 6 minutes. Quick-release pressure. A thermometer inserted in the chicken should read at least 165°.
2. Remove chicken. When cool enough to handle, shred meat with 2 forks; return to pressure cooker. Serve with rice and desired toppings.

¾ cup: 187 cal., 3g fat (1g sat. fat), 63mg chol., 1107mg sod., 11g carb. (2g sugars, 0 fiber), 23g pro.

TEST KITCHEN TIP
We love meal-in-one entrees served in bowls; but if that's not your thing, simply leave out the rice and wrap the chicken in a tortilla or pile it on a sandwich bun.

SAUSAGE FLORENTINE SHEPHERD'S PIE

Zesty tomatoes, Italian cheese blend and garlicky mashed potatoes make this dish long on flavor, even if the ingredient list is short.

—Leah Lyon, Ada, OK

Prep: 15 min.
Bake: 40 min. + standing
Makes: 6 servings

- 1 lb. bulk mild Italian sausage
- 1 can (14½ oz.) Italian diced tomatoes, lightly drained
- 1 pkg. (10 oz.) frozen chopped spinach, thawed and squeezed dry
- 3 cups shredded Italian cheese blend, divided
- 1 pkg. (24 oz.) refrigerated garlic mashed potatoes

1. Preheat oven to 375°. In a Dutch oven over medium heat, cook sausage, crumbling meat, until no longer pink, 5-6 minutes; drain. Stir in tomatoes, spinach and 2 cups cheese.
2. Pour sausage mixture into a greased 11x7-in. baking dish; top evenly with mashed potatoes. Bake 20 minutes; sprinkle with remaining cheese. Bake until cheese is melted and top begins to brown, about 20 minutes longer. Let stand 10 minutes before serving.

1 serving: 540 cal., 34g fat (16g sat. fat), 95mg chol., 1439mg sod., 23g carb. (6g sugars, 3g fiber), 24g pro.

SAUSAGE FLORENTINE SHEPHERD'S PIE

PULLED PORK PARFAIT

I tried a version of this meaty parfait at Miller Park, the then-home of my favorite baseball team, the Milwaukee Brewers. I take it up a notch by adding layers of corn and creamy mac and cheese. It truly is a full barbecue meal you can take on the go.

—Rachel Bernhard Seis, Milwaukee, WI

Takes: 15 min.
Makes: 4 servings

- 1 pkg. (16 oz.) refrigerated fully cooked barbecued shredded pork
- 1 cup frozen corn
- 2 cups refrigerated mashed potatoes
- 2 cups prepared macaroni and cheese

In each of four 1-pint wide-mouth canning jars, divide and layer ingredients in the following order: pulled pork, corn, mashed potatoes, and macaroni and cheese. Cover and refrigerate until ready to serve. When ready to serve, remove jar lids and microwave until heated through.

Freeze option: Cover prepared parfait jars and freeze. When ready to serve, partially thaw in refrigerator overnight before microwaving as directed.

1 serving: 349 cal., 8g fat (4g sat. fat), 45mg chol., 1116mg sod., 41g carb. (20g sugars, 1g fiber), 17g pro.

SAUSAGE & PEPPER PIEROGI SKILLET

SAUSAGE & PEPPER PIEROGI SKILLET

A package of pierogi lets me serve this tasty skillet meal in a hurry. The whole family really enjoys it.

—Molly Flessner, Bloomington, IL

Takes: 20 min.
Makes: 6 servings

- 1 pkg. (12.84 oz.) frozen mini four-cheese pierogi
- 2 Tbsp. olive oil, divided
- 1 lb. smoked turkey kielbasa, halved lengthwise and sliced diagonally
- 1 large sweet red pepper, cut into strips
- 1 medium onion, halved and sliced

1. Boil pierogi according to package directions; drain. Meanwhile, in a large skillet, heat 1 Tbsp. oil over medium heat. Add the kielbasa, pepper and onion; cook and stir until sausage is browned and onion is tender, 10-12 minutes. Remove from pan.

2. In same skillet, heat remaining oil over medium heat. Add the pierogi; cook and stir until lightly browned, 1-2 minutes. Return the kielbasa mixture to the pan; heat through.

1 serving: 257 cal., 10g fat (2g sat. fat), 52mg chol., 968mg sod., 24g carb. (7g sugars, 2g fiber), 16g pro.

GRILLED CHICKEN SAUSAGES WITH HARVEST RICE

GRILLED CHICKEN SAUSAGES WITH HARVEST RICE

Try something new on the grill tonight. My husband just loves chicken sausage, so I'm always creating new recipes to include it. We prefer the apple-flavored sausages, but any flavor would work well. Experiment to find your own personal favorite.

—Pamela Shank, Parkersburg, WV

Takes: 25 min.
Makes: 4 servings

- 1¾ cups chicken broth
- 2 cups instant brown rice
- 1 pkg. (12 oz.) frozen cooked winter squash, thawed and drained well
- ⅓ cup dried cranberries
- 1 pkg. (12 oz.) fully cooked apple chicken sausage links or flavor of your choice

1. Bring broth to a boil in a large saucepan. Stir in rice. Reduce heat; cover and simmer for 3 minutes. Add the squash and simmer, uncovered, for 4-6 minutes or until liquid is absorbed. Remove from the heat. Stir in cranberries; cover and let stand for 5 minutes.
2. Grill sausages, uncovered, over medium heat or broil 4 in. from the heat for 8-10 minutes or until heated through, turning often. Slice sausages and serve with rice mixture.

1 serving: 421 cal., 9g fat (2g sat. fat), 62mg chol., 911mg sod., 69g carb. (19g sugars, 5g fiber), 20g pro.

QUICK BEEF & NOODLES

My family loves this lighter version of beef Stroganoff. Using roast beef from the deli saves the hours spent cooking a whole roast. I serve it with a crisp green salad for a home-style meal.

—Pamela Shank, Parkersburg, WV

Takes: 25 min.
Makes: 2 servings

- 2½ cups uncooked yolk-free noodles
- ⅓ cup sliced fresh mushrooms
- ⅓ cup chopped onion
- 1 Tbsp. olive oil
- 1¼ cups reduced-sodium beef broth
- 6 oz. deli roast beef, cubed
- ⅛ tsp. pepper
- Optional: Sour cream and minced fresh parsley

1. Cook noodles according to package directions. In a large skillet, saute mushrooms and onion in oil until tender. Add broth, roast beef and pepper. Bring to a boil. Reduce heat; simmer, uncovered, for 10 minutes.
2. Drain noodles; stir into skillet. If desired, top with sour cream and parsley.

1½ cups: 375 cal., 10g fat (2g sat. fat), 50mg chol., 778mg sod., 42g carb. (5g sugars, 3g fiber), 26g pro. **Diabetic exchanges:** 3 starch, 3 lean meat, 1½ fat.

QUICK BEEF & NOODLES

SLOPPY JOE SPUDS

Five easy ingredients are all you need for these out-of-the-ordinary stuffed potatoes. Best of all, these tangy taters will be on your kitchen table in about 20 minutes.

—Nancee Melin, Tucson, AZ

Takes: 20 min.
Makes: 4 servings

- 4 large baking potatoes
- 1 lb. ground beef
- 1 can (16 oz.) bold sloppy joe sauce
- ½ cup shredded cheddar cheese
- 3 green onions, thinly sliced

1. Scrub and pierce potatoes; place on a microwave-safe plate. Microwave, uncovered, on high for 15-17 minutes or until tender, turning once.
2. Meanwhile, in a large skillet, cook beef over medium heat until no longer pink; drain. Stir in sloppy joe sauce; heat through.
3. Cut an "X" in the top of each potato; fluff pulp with a fork. Spoon meat mixture into potatoes; sprinkle with cheese and green onions.

1 serving: 627 cal., 15g fat (8g sat. fat), 71mg chol., 1370mg sod., 90g carb. (23g sugars, 8g fiber), 33g pro.

CREAMY SAUSAGE & BOW TIES

It's easy to jazz up a package of noodles for this savory and speedy supper. I stumbled across the recipe when I was running late for dinner. My kids love it!

—Linda Nilson, Melrose Park, IL

Takes: 25 min.
Makes: 4 servings

- 1 pkg. (4.1 oz.) four-cheese bow tie pasta mix
- ½ lb. fully cooked smoked sausage, cut into ¼-in. pieces
- 1 cup frozen peas
- 1 cup shredded part-skim mozzarella cheese

Prepare the pasta mix according to the package directions. Meanwhile, in a large skillet, brown sausage; drain. Add the peas and pasta. Simmer, uncovered, for 1-2 minutes or until heated through. Sprinkle with the cheese. Cover and cook for 1-2 minutes or until the cheese is melted.

1 cup: 387 cal., 22g fat (10g sat. fat), 59mg chol., 1199mg sod., 26g carb. (5g sugars, 2g fiber), 21g pro.

CREAMY SAUSAGE & BOW TIES

HAM & CHEESE POTATO CASSEROLE

This recipe makes two cheesy, delicious casseroles. Have one tonight and put the other on ice for a future busy weeknight. It's like having money in the bank when things get hectic!

—Kari Adams, Fort Collins, CO

Prep: 15 min.
Bake: 50 min. + standing
Makes: 2 casseroles (5 servings each)

- 2 cans (10¾ oz. each) condensed cream of celery soup, undiluted
- 2 cups sour cream
- ½ cup water
- ½ tsp. pepper
- 2 pkg. (28 oz. each) frozen O'Brien potatoes
- 1 pkg. (16 oz.) process cheese (Velveeta), cubed
- 2½ cups cubed fully cooked ham

1. Preheat oven to 375°. In a large bowl, mix the soup, sour cream, water and pepper until blended. Stir in potatoes, cheese and ham.

2. Transfer to 2 greased 2-qt. baking dishes. Bake, covered, 40 minutes. Uncover; bake 10-15 minutes longer or until bubbly. Let stand 10 minutes before serving.

Freeze option: Cover and freeze the unbaked casseroles. To use, partially thaw in refrigerator overnight. Remove from the refrigerator 30 minutes before baking. Preheat oven to 375°. Bake the casseroles as directed, increasing the baking time as necessary to heat through and for a thermometer inserted in center to read 165°.

1⅓ cups: 474 cal., 26g fat (14g sat. fat), 92mg chol., 1555mg sod., 36g carb. (7g sugars, 4g fiber), 20g pro.

STEAK & POTATO FOIL PACKS

STEAK & POTATO FOIL PACKS

As a park ranger, I've cooked a lot of meals outdoors. I often assemble foil packs and toss them into my backpack with some ice. Then when I set up camp, it's easy to cook them over a campfire. If I'm at home, I use my grill, and the food is just as tasty.

—Ralph Jones, San Diego, CA

Prep: 20 min. • **Grill:** 20 min.
Makes: 8 servings

- 2 beef top sirloin steaks (1½ lbs. each)
- 3 lbs. red potatoes, cut into ½-in. cubes
- 1 medium onion, chopped
- 4 tsp. minced fresh rosemary
- 1 Tbsp. minced garlic
- 2 tsp. salt
- 1 tsp. pepper

1. Prepare grill for medium heat or preheat oven to 450°. Cut each steak into 4 pieces, for a total of 8 pieces. In a large bowl, combine steak, potatoes, onion, rosemary, garlic, salt and pepper.
2. Divide mixture among eight 18x12-in. pieces of heavy-duty foil, placing food on dull side of foil. Fold foil around potato mixture, sealing tightly.
3. Place packets on grill or in oven; cook until potatoes are tender, 8-10 minutes on each side. Open the packets carefully to allow any steam to escape. If desired, sprinkle with additional rosemary.

1 packet: 348 cal., 7g fat (3g sat. fat), 69mg chol., 677mg sod., 29g carb. (2g sugars, 3g fiber), 40g pro. **Diabetic exchanges:** 5 lean meat, 2 starch.

REUBEN PIZZA

Fridays are pizza nights at our house, and we like to do a lot of experimenting so we don't have the same old thing every single week. With only five ingredients, this pizza is a snap to whip up—and it tastes just like a Reuben sandwich.

—Nicole German, Hutchinson, MN

Takes: 25 min.
Makes: 6 servings

- 1 prebaked 12-in. pizza crust
- ⅔ cup Thousand Island salad dressing
- ½ lb. sliced deli corned beef, cut into strips
- 1 can (14 oz.) sauerkraut, rinsed and well drained
- 2 cups shredded Swiss cheese

Preheat oven to 400°. Place the crust on an ungreased or parchment-lined baking sheet. Spread with salad dressing. Top with corned beef, sauerkraut and cheese. Bake until cheese is melted, 12-15 minutes.

1 piece: 480 cal., 27g fat (10g sat. fat), 57mg chol., 1527mg sod., 36g carb. (6g sugars, 3g fiber), 23g pro.

REUBEN PIZZA

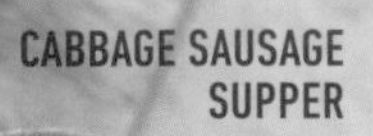
CABBAGE SAUSAGE SUPPER

CABBAGE SAUSAGE SUPPER

Everyone is surprised at how this flavorful combination calls for just a few ingredients. I complete the meal with a no-bake fruit dessert.
—Ruby Williams, Bogalusa, LA

Prep: 10 min. • **Cook:** 40 min.
Makes: 12 servings

- 2 lbs. smoked sausage, halved and cut into ¾-in. slices
- 1 large onion, cut into eighths
- 1 medium head cabbage, chopped
- ½ cup water
- 1 lb. carrots, cut into ½-in. slices
- 5 medium potatoes, peeled and cut into ¾-in. cubes

In a Dutch oven or soup kettle, cook sausage and onion over medium heat until sausage is lightly browned and onion is tender; drain. Add the cabbage and water. Cover and cook on low for 10 minutes. Stir in the carrots and potatoes. Cover and cook for 25-30 minutes or until the vegetables are tender.
1¼ cups: 190 cal., 4g fat (1g sat. fat), 34mg chol., 675mg sod., 28g carb. (0 sugars, 4g fiber), 13g pro. **Diabetic exchanges:** 2 starch, 1 lean meat.

PESTO CHICKEN & ASPARAGUS

PESTO CHICKEN & ASPARAGUS

With only five items, I can put a beautiful meal on the table in very little time. I use store-bought pesto, which makes preparation easy. This skillet dish is the only way I can get my toddler to eat asparagus.
—Brooke Icenhour, Easley, SC

Takes: 30 min.
Makes: 4 servings

- 1 lb. boneless skinless chicken breasts, cut into 1-in. cubes
- 1 Tbsp. olive oil
- 1 lb. fresh asparagus, trimmed and cut into 1-in. pieces
- 1 cup heavy whipping cream
- ½ cup prepared pesto
- ⅛ tsp. pepper
- Hot cooked couscous

In a large skillet, saute chicken in oil until no longer pink. Remove and set aside. In the same skillet, saute asparagus until crisp-tender. Stir in the cream, pesto and pepper until blended. Return chicken to the pan; heat through. Serve with couscous.
1 cup: 525 cal., 42g fat (19g sat. fat), 154mg chol., 321mg sod., 6g carb. (1g sugars, 2g fiber), 31g pro.

BEEF TERIYAKI NOODLES

BEEF TERIYAKI NOODLES

At our house, we love to combine fresh ingredients with a pantry product. Our version of this recipe starts with beef, onions, peppers and mushrooms, since we always have them on hand, but you can make the dish your own!
—Richard Robinson, Park Forest, IL

Takes: 20 min.
Makes: 4 servings

- 1 envelope (4.6 oz.) lo mein noodles and teriyaki sauce mix
- 1 lb. beef flat iron steak or top sirloin steak, cut into bite-sized pieces
- ¼ tsp. salt
- ¼ tsp. pepper
- 2 Tbsp. canola oil, divided
- 2 cups frozen pepper and onion stir-fry blend
- 1 cup sliced fresh mushrooms

1. Prepare noodle mix according to package directions.
2. Meanwhile, sprinkle beef with salt and pepper. In a large skillet, heat 1 Tbsp. oil over medium-high heat. Add beef; stir-fry 6-8 minutes or until no longer pink. Remove from pan; discard the drippings.
3. Stir-fry vegetable blend and mushrooms in the remaining oil 3-4 minutes or until vegetables are tender.
4. Return beef to pan. Stir in noodle mixture; heat through.

1 cup: 403 cal., 20g fat (5g sat. fat), 73mg chol., 541mg sod., 28g carb. (3g sugars, 2g fiber), 24g pro.

BAKED TERIYAKI PORK & VEGGIES

Minimal preparation makes this dish easy. I use precut broccoli and boneless, trimmed pork chops to save time. Sometimes I throw in multicolored carrots for extra flair. Try it served over rice or even noodles.

—Billie Davis, Spring Creek, NV

Prep: 15 min. • **Bake:** 30 min.
Makes: 4 servings

- 2 cups fresh broccoli florets
- 1 lb. fresh baby carrots, halved lengthwise
- 1 Tbsp. olive oil
- 1 tsp. minced fresh gingerroot
- ½ tsp. pepper
- ¼ tsp. salt
- 4 boneless pork loin chops (6 oz. each)
- 4 Tbsp. reduced-sodium teriyaki sauce
- Toasted sesame seeds, optional

1. Preheat oven to 375°. Line a 15x10x1-in. pan with foil; add broccoli and carrots. Toss with olive oil, ginger, pepper and salt; spread out into a single layer.
2. Place pork chops on top of vegetables; drizzle with teriyaki sauce. Bake until a thermometer inserted in pork reads 145°, about 30 minutes. If desired, preheat broiler; broil chops and vegetables 2-4 in. from heat until browned, 1-2 minutes. Top with sesame seeds if desired.

1 pork chop with 1 cup vegetables: 322 cal., 13g fat (4g sat. fat), 82mg chol., 613mg sod., 14g carb. (9g sugars, 3g fiber), 35g pro. **Diabetic exchanges:** 5 lean meat, 2 vegetable, ½ fat.

BAKED TERIYAKI PORK & VEGGIES

BEEFY TORTELLINI SKILLET

BEEFY TORTELLINI SKILLET

This skillet wonder is a tortellini dish the family craves. From browning beef to cooking the pasta and melting the cheese, everything happens in one pan. You can add basil or chives for a touch of freshness.

—Juli Meyers, Hinesville, GA

Takes: 20 min.
Makes: 4 servings

- 1 lb. ground beef
- ½ tsp. Montreal steak seasoning
- 1 cup water
- 1 tsp. beef bouillon granules
- 1 pkg. (19 oz.) frozen cheese tortellini
- 1 cup shredded Italian cheese blend

1. In a large skillet, cook beef over medium heat until no longer pink, 5-6 minutes; crumble meat; drain. Stir in steak seasoning. Add water and bouillon; bring to a boil. Stir in tortellini; return to a boil. Reduce heat; simmer, covered until tortellini are tender, 3-4 minutes.
2. Remove from heat; sprinkle with cheese. Let stand, covered, until cheese is melted.

1½ cups: 566 cal., 28g fat (13g sat. fat), 111mg chol., 899mg sod., 37g carb. (2g sugars, 2g fiber), 39g pro.

MEXICAN BUBBLE PIZZA

This tasty pizza offers a new way to experience Mexican cuisine. Serve it at your next party and watch it disappear!
—Jackie Hannahs,
Cedar Springs, MI

Prep: 15 min.
Cook: 3 hours 5 min.
Makes: 6 servings

- 1½ lbs. ground beef
- 1 can (10¾ oz.) condensed tomato soup, undiluted
- ¾ cup water
- 1 envelope taco seasoning
- 1 tube (16.3 oz.) large refrigerated buttermilk biscuits
- 2 cups shredded cheddar cheese
- Optional toppings: Shredded lettuce, chopped tomatoes, salsa, sliced ripe olives, sour cream and thinly sliced green onions

1. Line a 6-qt. slow cooker with a double thickness of heavy-duty foil. Coat with cooking spray.
2. In a large skillet, cook the beef over medium heat until no longer pink, 6-8 minutes, breaking into crumbles; drain. Stir in soup, water and taco seasoning. Bring mixture to a boil. Reduce heat; simmer, uncovered, until slightly thickened, 3-5 minutes.
3. Cut each biscuit into 4 pieces; gently stir into beef mixture. Transfer to slow cooker. Cook, covered, on low until dough is cooked through, 3-4 hours. Sprinkle with cheese. Cook, covered, until cheese is melted, about 5 minutes longer. Serve with toppings of your choice.

1 serving: 643 cal., 35g fat (15g sat. fat), 109mg chol., 1870mg sod., 46g carb. (8g sugars, 2g fiber), 35g pro.

TEST KITCHEN TIPS

The foil liner does double duty. Not only does it make cleanup a breeze, but it prevents hot spots that can burn the edges of the pizza. The meat mixture can be made 2 or 3 days in advance. Just rewarm it before stirring in biscuits. To easily turn up the heat, simply use pepper jack cheese instead of cheddar.

HOME-STYLE STEW

HOME-STYLE STEW

My husband and I both work full time, so quick meals are important. Because this stew always tastes great, it's a regular menu item for us.
—Marie Shanks, Terre Haute, IN

Prep: 20 min. • **Cook:** 6 hours
Makes: 5 servings

- 2 pkg. (16 oz. each) frozen vegetables for stew
- 1½ lbs. beef stew meat, cut into 1-in. cubes
- 1 can (10¾ oz.) condensed cream of mushroom soup, undiluted
- 1 can (10¾ oz.) condensed tomato soup, undiluted
- 1 envelope reduced-sodium onion soup mix

1. Place vegetables in a 5-qt. slow cooker. In a large skillet coated with cooking spray, brown beef on all sides.
2. Transfer to slow cooker. Combine the remaining ingredients; pour over the top.
3. Cover and cook on low for 6-8 hours or until meat is tender.

1½ cups: 404 cal., 13g fat (4g sat. fat), 87mg chol., 1025mg sod., 39g carb. (9g sugars, 4g fiber), 30g pro.

CURRY SHRIMP LINGUINE

Curry, cilantro and coconut milk make this dish an exciting change of pace. Also try it with rice noodles or spaghetti.
—Jana Rippee, Casa Grande, AZ

Takes: 25 min.
Makes: 6 servings

- 1 pkg. (16 oz.) linguine
- 3 tsp. curry powder
- 1 can (13.66 oz.) light coconut milk
- ½ tsp. salt
- ¼ tsp. pepper
- 1¼ lbs. uncooked medium shrimp, peeled and deveined
- ⅓ cup minced fresh cilantro

1. Cook linguine according to package directions. Meanwhile, in a large skillet over medium heat, toast curry powder for 2 minutes, stirring frequently. Stir in the milk, salt and pepper.
2. Bring to a boil. Add shrimp; cook until the shrimp turn pink, 5-6 minutes. Drain the linguine; toss with the shrimp mixture and cilantro.

1½ cups: 406 cal., 8g fat (4g sat. fat), 115mg chol., 313mg sod., 58g carb. (4g sugars, 3g fiber), 26g pro.

CURRY SHRIMP LINGUINE

SLOPPY JOE HOT DISH

Dinner will be served in no time with this kid-friendly supper. Get little ones involved by letting them stir together the meaty filling and spoon it onto the crust.

—Marlene Harguth, Maynard, MN

Prep: 15 min. • **Bake:** 20 min.
Makes: 6 servings

- 1 pkg. (8 oz.) refrigerated crescent rolls
- 1 lb. ground beef
- 1 can (15 oz.) tomato sauce
- 1 envelope sloppy joe mix
- 1 cup shredded part-skim mozzarella cheese

1. Unroll crescent dough into 2 rectangles; seal seams and perforations. Roll out each rectangle between 2 pieces of waxed paper to fit an 11x7-in. baking dish.
2. Grease the dish and place 1 rectangle inside. Bake at 425° for 5 minutes or until golden brown.
3. Meanwhile, in a large skillet, cook beef over medium heat until no longer pink; drain. Stir in the tomato sauce and sloppy joe mix; spoon over crust. Sprinkle with cheese; top with remaining dough. Bake 15-20 minutes longer or until golden brown.

1 piece: 363 cal., 20g fat (8g sat. fat), 59mg chol., 1245mg sod., 25g carb. (6g sugars, 1g fiber), 22g pro.

GRILLED ASIAN SALMON PACKETS

I don't like plain salmon, but this has a nice stir-fried flavor!

—Janice Miller, Creston, IA

Takes: 25 min.
Makes: 4 servings

- 4 salmon fillets (6 oz. each)
- 3 cups fresh sugar snap peas
- 1 small sweet red pepper, cut into strips
- 1 small sweet yellow pepper, cut into strips
- ¼ cup reduced-fat Asian toasted sesame salad dressing

1. Place each salmon fillet on a double thickness of heavy-duty foil (about 12 in. square). Combine sugar snap peas and peppers; spoon over salmon. Drizzle with salad dressing. Fold foil around mixture and seal tightly.
2. Grill, covered, over medium heat for 15-20 minutes or until fish flakes easily with a fork. Open foil carefully to allow steam to escape.

1 salmon fillet with 1 cup vegetables: 350 cal., 17g fat (3g sat. fat), 85mg chol., 237mg sod., 14g carb. (9g sugars, 4g fiber), 34g pro. **Diabetic exchanges:** 4 lean meat, 2 vegetable, 2 fat.

GRILLED ASIAN SALMON PACKETS

CHEESY CHICKEN & BROCCOLI ORZO

CHEESY CHICKEN & BROCCOLI ORZO

Broccoli-rice casserole tops my family's list of favorites. When we need dinner fast, this stovetop dish is usually what I turn to. Orzo and frozen veggies make it quick and easy.
—Mary Shivers, Ada, OK

Takes: 30 min.
Makes: 6 servings

- 1¼ cups uncooked orzo pasta
- 2 pkg. (10 oz. each) frozen broccoli with cheese sauce
- 2 Tbsp. butter
- 1½ lbs. boneless skinless chicken breasts, cut into ½-in. cubes
- 1 medium onion, chopped
- ¾ tsp. salt
- ½ tsp. pepper

1. Cook the orzo according to package directions. Meanwhile, heat broccoli with cheese sauce according to package directions.
2. In a large skillet, heat butter over medium heat. Add chicken, onion, salt and pepper; cook and stir 6-8 minutes or until chicken is no longer pink and onion is tender. Drain orzo. Stir orzo and broccoli with cheese sauce into skillet; heat through.

1 cup: 359 cal., 9g fat (4g sat. fat), 77mg chol., 655mg sod., 38g carb. (4g sugars, 3g fiber), 30g pro. **Diabetic exchanges:** 3 lean meat, 2 starch, 1 vegetable, 1 fat.

★★★★★ READER REVIEW

"This was easy and tasty. I used a store-bought cooked chicken to save even more time."
—RENAGAM, TASTEOFHOME.COM

HAM & SPINACH CASSEROLE

This is down-home cooking at its best! Ham and veggies join forces with a creamy sauce and pretty topping to create a hearty meal-in-one.

—*Taste of Home* Test Kitchen

Prep: 25 min. • **Bake:** 20 min.
Makes: 4 servings

- 3 cups cubed fully cooked ham
- 1 pkg. (16 oz.) frozen sliced carrots, thawed
- 1 can (10¾ oz.) condensed cream of potato soup, undiluted
- 1 pkg. (10 oz.) frozen creamed spinach, thawed
- ¼ cup water
- ¼ tsp. pepper
- ⅛ tsp. salt
- 1 tube (4 oz.) refrigerated crescent rolls

1. In a large skillet coated with cooking spray, cook the ham over medium heat until lightly browned. Stir in the carrots, soup, spinach, water, pepper and salt; heat through. Pour mixture into a greased 8-in. square baking dish.
2. Unroll the crescent dough; separate into 2 rectangles. Seal perforations. Cut each rectangle lengthwise into 4 strips; make a lattice crust over ham mixture. Bake at 375° until the filling is bubbly and the crust is golden brown, 18-22 minutes.

1 serving: 376 cal., 13g fat (3g sat. fat), 65mg chol., 2334mg sod., 37g carb. (11g sugars, 6g fiber), 28g pro.

SAUCY RANCH PORK & POTATOES

My sister shared a roast recipe, and I tweaked it into this dish using items I had on hand.

—Kendra Adamson, Layton, UT

Prep: 20 min. • **Cook:** 4 hours
Makes: 6 servings

- 2 lbs. red potatoes (about 6 medium), cut into ¾-in. cubes
- ¼ cup water
- 6 boneless pork loin chops (6 oz. each)
- 2 cans (10¾ oz. each) condensed cream of chicken soup, undiluted
- 1 cup 2% milk
- 1 envelope ranch salad dressing mix
- Minced fresh parsley, optional

1. Place potatoes and water in a large microwave-safe dish. Microwave, covered, on high for 3-5 minutes or until potatoes are almost tender; drain.
2. Transfer potatoes and pork to a 4- or 5-qt. slow cooker. In a bowl, mix condensed soup, milk and salad dressing mix; pour over pork chops. Cook, covered, on low 4-5 hours or until the pork and potatoes are tender (a thermometer inserted in pork should read at least 145°). If desired, sprinkle with parsley.

1 pork chop with ¾ cup potatoes and ½ cup sauce: 468 cal., 17g fat (6g sat. fat), 94mg chol., 1189mg sod., 37g carb. (4g sugars, 4g fiber), 39g pro.

SAUCY RANCH PORK & POTATOES

WARM CHICKEN
TORTELLINI AU GRATIN

WARM CHICKEN TORTELLINI AU GRATIN

I have a number of quick and easy planned leftover meals in my recipe arsenal. They come in handy during the holiday season, when people are coming and going (and staying!), and I'm always busy. This is one of my favorites; pasta from Monday plus roasted chicken from Tuesday equals this delicious dish on Wednesday. Paired with a green salad, it is a meal that's fancy enough for company.
—Brenda Cole, Reisterstown, MD

Prep: 15 min. • **Bake:** 30 min.
Makes: 6 servings

- 2 cans (14 oz. each) water-packed artichoke hearts
- 3 cups shredded cooked chicken
- 3 cups refrigerated spinach tortellini, cooked
- 1½ cups mayonnaise
- 1½ cups grated Asiago cheese, divided
- Fresh basil, optional

1. Preheat oven to 350°. Drain artichoke hearts, reserving ¼ cup of juices. Coarsely chop; combine with chicken, tortellini, mayonnaise, 1 cup cheese and reserved artichoke liquid. Place artichoke mixture in a greased 13x9-in. baking dish; sprinkle with remaining cheese.
2. Bake until bubbly and starting to brown, about 30 minutes. If desired, garnish with basil.

1⅓ cups: 709 cal., 54g fat (13g sat. fat), 101mg chol., 859mg sod., 19g carb. (1g sugars, 2g fiber), 34g pro.

BEEF TIP STEW OVER FUSILLI

BEEF TIP STEW OVER FUSILLI

Fire-roasted tomatoes add color and flair to this entree with a tasty veggie blend.
—*Taste of Home* Test Kitchen

Takes: 25 min.
Makes: 4 servings

- 2½ cups uncooked fusilli pasta
- 1 pkg. (17 oz.) refrigerated beef tips with gravy
- 1 pkg. (12 oz.) frozen garlic baby peas and mushrooms blend
- 1 can (14½ oz.) fire-roasted diced tomatoes, undrained
- ½ tsp. dried thyme
- ¼ tsp. pepper

Cook pasta according to package directions. Meanwhile, in a large skillet, combine the beef tips with gravy, vegetable blend, tomatoes, thyme and pepper; heat through. Drain pasta. Serve with beef mixture.

1 cup beef mixture with 1 cup pasta: 451 cal., 9g fat (2g sat. fat), 47mg chol., 1258mg sod., 64g carb. (11g sugars, 7g fiber), 30g pro.

BEEFY FAVORITES

BALSAMIC-GLAZED BEEF SKEWERS
P. 73

WHEN IT'S DINNER TIME, BEEF IS ALWAYS A SUREFIRE BET. TURN HERE TO SATISFY THE MEAT-AND-POTATOES LOVERS IN YOUR HOME.

EASY MARINATED GRILLED FLANK STEAK

EASY MARINATED GRILLED FLANK STEAK

Friends shared this three-ingredient marinade years ago, and it's been a favorite ever since. Serve the steak with salad and grilled potatoes for a quick meal.

—Beverly Dietz, Surprise, AZ

Prep: 5 min. + marinating
Grill: 15 min. • **Makes:** 8 servings

- 1 cup barbecue sauce
- ½ cup burgundy wine or beef broth
- ¼ cup lemon juice
- 1 beef flank steak (2 lbs.)

1. In a small bowl, whisk the barbecue sauce, wine and lemon juice until blended. Pour 1 cup marinade into a shallow dish. Add beef and turn to coat. Cover; refrigerate 4 hours or overnight. Cover and refrigerate the remaining marinade.
2. Drain the beef, discarding the marinade in dish. Grill steak, covered, over medium heat until meat reaches desired doneness (for medium-rare, a thermometer should read 135°; medium, 140°; medium-well, 145°), 6-8 minutes on each side. Let stand 5 minutes before thinly slicing across the grain. Serve with reserved marinade.

3 oz. cooked steak with 1½ Tbsp. reserved marinade : 195 cal., 9g fat (4g sat. fat), 54mg chol., 271mg sod., 4g carb. (3g sugars, 0 fiber), 22g pro. **Diabetic exchanges:** 3 lean meat, 1 fat.

COCONUT MANGO THAI BEEF CURRY

My recipe provides a lot of sweet heat. The mango and coconut milk taste tropical while the curry paste adds a little fire. To make a milder dish, just reduce the amount of curry paste.

—Terri Lynn Merritts, Nashville, TN

Prep: 10 min. • **Cook:** 2¼ hours
Makes: 6 servings

- 2 Tbsp. peanut oil or canola oil
- 3 Tbsp. red curry paste
- 2½ cups coconut milk
- 2½ lbs. boneless beef chuck roast, cut into 1-in. cubes
- 1 cup dried mango, chopped
- 1 tsp. salt
- ¼ tsp. pepper
- Optional: Hot cooked rice, sliced red onions, fresh cilantro and lime wedges

1. In a Dutch oven, heat peanut oil over low heat. Add curry paste; cook and stir 3-5 minutes. Add coconut milk; cook and stir 3-5 minutes longer.
2. Stir in beef, mango, salt and pepper. Increase heat to medium-high; bring to a boil. Reduce the heat; simmer, uncovered, stirring occasionally, until the meat is tender, about 2 hours. If desired, serve with rice, onions, fresh cilantro and lime wedges.

1 cup: 578 cal., 38g fat (23g sat. fat), 123mg chol., 793mg sod., 17g carb. (14g sugars, 1g fiber), 39g pro.

COCONUT MANGO THAI
BEEF CURRY

TEXAS-STYLE BRISKET

This is the quintessential brisket here in the Lone Star State. Even my husband's six-generation Texas family is impressed! Grilling with wood chips takes a little extra effort, but I promise, you'll be glad you did. Each bite tastes like heaven on a plate.

—Renee Morgan, Taylor, TX

Prep: 35 min. + chilling
Cook: 6 hours + standing
Makes: 20 servings

- 1 whole fresh beef brisket (12 to 14 lbs.)
- ½ cup pepper
- ¼ cup kosher salt
- Large disposable foil pan
- About 6 cups wood chips, preferably oak

1. Trim fat on brisket to ½-in. thickness. Rub brisket with pepper and salt; place in a large disposable foil pan, fat side up. Refrigerate, covered, several hours or overnight. Meanwhile, soak wood chips in water.

2. To prepare grill for slow indirect cooking, adjust grill vents so top vent is half open and bottom vent is open only a quarter of the way. Make 2 arrangements of 45 unlit coals on opposite sides of the grill, leaving the center of the grill open. Light 20 additional coals until ash-covered; distribute over unlit coals. Sprinkle 2 cups soaked wood chips over lit coals.

3. Replace grill rack. Close grill and allow temperature in grill to reach 275°, about 15 minutes.

4. Place foil pan with brisket in center of grill rack; cover grill and cook 3 hours (do not open grill). Check temperature of the grill periodically to maintain a temperature of 275° throughout cooking. The heat level may be adjusted by opening the vents to raise the temperature and closing the vents partway to decrease temperature.

5. Add another 10 unlit coals and 1 cup wood chips to each side of the grill. Cook brisket, covered, 3-4 hours longer or until fork-tender (a thermometer inserted in brisket should read about 190°); add coals and wood chips as needed to maintain a grill temperature of 275°.

6. Remove brisket from grill. Cover tightly with foil; let stand 30-60 minutes. Cut brisket across the grain into slices.

5 oz. cooked beef: 351 cal., 12g fat (4g sat. fat), 116mg chol., 1243mg sod., 2g carb. (0 sugars, 1g fiber), 56g pro.

TEST KITCHEN TIP
If your charcoal grill doesn't have a built-in thermometer, the grill temperature may be checked by simply inserting the stem of a food thermometer through the top vent.

TEXAS-STYLE BRISKET

CARIBBEAN GRILLED RIBEYES

CARIBBEAN GRILLED RIBEYES

I made this mind-blowing steak with my father-in-law in mind. He loved it, and so did everyone else. You can serve it for casual suppers or more elaborate parties on the weekend.

—De'Lawrence Reed, Durham, NC

Prep: 10 min. + marinating
Grill: 10 min. • **Makes:** 4 servings

- ½ cup Dr Pepper
- 3 Tbsp. honey
- ¼ cup Caribbean jerk seasoning
- 1½ tsp. chopped seeded habanero pepper
- ½ tsp. salt
- ½ tsp. pepper
- 4 beef ribeye steaks (¾ lb. each)

1. Place the first 6 ingredients in a blender; cover and process until blended. Pour into a shallow bowl. Add steaks; turn to coat. Cover and refrigerate at least 2 hours.

2. Drain steaks, discarding the marinade. Grill steaks, covered, over medium heat or broil 3-4 in. from heat for 4-6 minutes on each side or until meat reaches desired doneness (for medium-rare, a thermometer should read 135°; medium, 140°; medium-well, 145°).

1 steak: 762 cal., 54g fat (22g sat. fat), 202mg chol., 442mg sod., 4g carb. (4g sugars, 0 fiber), 61g pro.

CRAB & HERB CHEESE FILET MIGNON

CRAB & HERB CHEESE FILET MIGNON

Save the money you'd spend on going out for surf and turf. Instead, treat yourselves to thick-cut steaks stuffed with garlic-herb cheese spread and fresh crabmeat. It's a home-cooked entree that looks and tastes like it came from a four-star restaurant!

—*Taste of Home* Test Kitchen

Prep: 15 min. • **Broil:** 20 min.
Makes: 4 servings

- 1½ cups fresh crabmeat
- 1 pkg. (6½ oz.) garlic-herb spreadable cheese, divided
- 4 beef tenderloin steaks (1 in. thick and 8 oz. each)
- ¼ tsp. salt
- ¼ tsp. pepper

1. Combine crab and ¾ cup spreadable cheese in a small bowl. Cut a horizontal pocket in each steak. Fill each pocket with ⅓ cup crab mixture. Place steaks on a greased broiler pan. Sprinkle with salt and pepper.

2. Broil 4 in. from the heat for 10 minutes on each side or until the meat reaches desired doneness (for medium-rare, a thermometer should read 135°; medium, 140°; medium-well, 145°), spooning the remaining cheese over steaks during the last 2 minutes of broiling. Let stand for at least 5 minutes before serving.

1 stuffed steak: 558 cal., 34g fat (19g sat. fat), 197mg chol., 547mg sod., 2g carb. (0 sugars, 0 fiber), 60g pro.

COWBOY STEW

I made up this dish back in the early 1970s when I was down to very little food in the house. Since it's a combination of barbecue sauce, hamburger, hot dogs and beans, this one-skillet meal makes both children and adults happy.

—Val Rananawski, Millville, NJ

Takes: 30 min.
Makes: 11 servings

- 2 lbs. ground beef
- 4 cans (16 oz. each) baked beans
- 8 hot dogs, sliced
- ½ cup barbecue sauce
- ½ cup grated Parmesan cheese
- Optional: chopped green onions

In a Dutch oven, cook the beef over medium heat until no longer pink; drain. Stir in the remaining ingredients. Bring to a boil. Reduce heat; cover and simmer for 4-6 minutes or until flavors are blended. Serve with green onions if desired.

1 cup: 469 cal., 23g fat (9g sat. fat), 84mg chol., 1256mg sod., 39g carb. (5g sugars, 9g fiber), 28g pro.

TEST KITCHEN TIP
Pare down the fat in this dish by replacing the ground beef with ground turkey and leaving out the cheese altogether.

COWBOY STEW

FRUITED POT ROAST

FRUITED POT ROAST

Here's a wonderful variation of classic pot roast. The fruit is a change from the vegetables that usually accompany this dish. My family really enjoys it.
—Linda South, Pineville, NC

Prep: 15 min. • **Cook:** 6 hours
Makes: 6 servings

- 1 pkg. (7 oz.) mixed dried fruit
- 1 large onion, cut into wedges
- 1 can (5½ oz.) unsweetened apple juice
- 1 boneless beef chuck roast (2 lbs.)
- ½ tsp. salt
- ¼ tsp. ground allspice
- ¼ tsp. pepper

1. Place the fruit and onion in a 3- or 4-qt. slow cooker; add the apple juice. Top with roast; sprinkle with the seasonings.
2. Cover and cook on low until meat is tender, 6-8 hours. Serve beef with fruit mixture.

4 oz. cooked beef with ½ cup fruit mixture: 394 cal., 15g fat (6g sat. fat), 98mg chol., 302mg sod., 32g carb. (28g sugars, 2g fiber), 30g pro.

CHILI-BEER GLAZED STEAKS

CHILI-BEER GLAZED STEAKS

Bold ingredients give these tender grilled steaks a taste you won't soon forget. We loved the slightly sweet and pleasantly smoky glaze. Get ready to make mouths water!
—Geordyth Sullivan, Cutler Bay, FL

Prep: 25 min. • **Grill:** 10 min.
Makes: 4 servings

- ⅔ cup chili sauce
- ⅔ cup spicy steak sauce
- ½ cup chopped shallots
- ½ cup beer or nonalcoholic beer
- 4 boneless beef top loin steaks (8 oz. each)
- ½ tsp. salt
- ½ tsp. pepper

1. In a small saucepan, combine the chili sauce, steak sauce, shallots and beer. Bring to a boil. Reduce the heat; simmer, uncovered, for 12-15 minutes or until slightly thickened. Set aside ½ cup for serving and keep warm. Sprinkle steaks with salt and pepper.
2. Lightly oil the grill rack. Grill steaks, covered, over medium heat or broil 4 in. from the heat for 4-6 minutes on each side or until meat reaches desired doneness (for medium-rare, a thermometer should read 135°; medium, 140°; medium-well, 145°), basting occasionally with sauce mixture. Serve with reserved sauce.

1 steak with 2 Tbsp. sauce: 398 cal., 10g fat (4g sat. fat), 100mg chol., 1757mg sod., 23g carb (14g sugars, 0 fiber), 49g pro.

FAST PHILLY CHEESESTEAK PIZZA

Cheesesteaks and pizza are such favorites, I just had to combine them. We top a pizza crust with roast beef, cheese, onions and peppers for a hand-held feast.

—Jackie Hannahs,
Cedar Springs, MI

Takes: 30 min. • **Makes:** 6 pieces

- 1 tube (13.8 oz.) refrigerated pizza crust
- 2 cups frozen pepper and onion stir-fry blend
- 2 Tbsp. Dijon-mayonnaise blend
- ½ lb. thinly sliced deli roast beef, cut into wide strips
- 1½ cups shredded cheddar cheese

1. Preheat oven to 425°. Grease a 12-in. pizza pan. Unroll and press pizza dough into the pan. Pinch edge to form a rim. Bake 8-10 minutes or until edge is lightly browned.

2. Meanwhile, place a large skillet coated with cooking spray over medium-high heat. Add the stir-fry blend; cook and stir until heated through, 3-5 minutes.

3. Spread mayonnaise blend over crust; top with roast beef and vegetables. Sprinkle with cheese. Bake 10-15 minutes or until cheese is melted.

1 piece: 330 cal., 13g fat (7g sat. fat), 51mg chol., 983mg sod., 34g carb. (6g sugars, 1g fiber), 20g pro.

TENDERLOIN WITH HORSERADISH CREAM CHEESE

My husband and I both love the classic combination of beef and horseradish. Baked potatoes make a great side dish.

—Mary Lou Cook, Welches, OR

Takes: 20 min. **Makes:** 4 servings

- 4 beef tenderloin steaks (4 oz. each)
- ¼ tsp. salt
- ¼ tsp. pepper
- 1 tsp. olive oil
- 1 pkg. (8 oz.) cream cheese, softened
- 2 Tbsp. grated Parmesan cheese
- 2 Tbsp. prepared horseradish
- 2 Tbsp. minced fresh parsley

1. Sprinkle the steaks with salt and pepper. In a large skillet, heat olive oil over medium heat. Add steaks; cook 4-6 minutes on each side or until meat reaches desired doneness (for medium-rare, a thermometer should read 135°; medium, 140°; medium-well, 145°).

2. Meanwhile, in a small bowl, mix cream cheese, Parmesan cheese and horseradish until blended. Serve with steaks. Sprinkle with parsley.

1 steak with ¼ cup topping: 387 cal., 28g fat (16g sat. fat), 114mg chol., 378mg sod., 3g carb. (1g sugars, 0 fiber), 30g pro.

TENDERLOIN WITH HORSERADISH CREAM CHEESE

TEX-MEX MACARONI

My husband and I really like macaroni and cheese. When we had a lot left over on one occasion, I came up with this Tex-Mex version to use it up. This quick casserole is very good with a green salad.

—Arlene Lacell, Zillah, WA

Prep: 10 min. • **Bake:** 25 min.
Makes: 4 servings

- ½ lb. ground beef
- ½ cup chopped onion
- 3 cups prepared macaroni and cheese
- 1 cup salsa
- ½ cup shredded cheddar cheese

1. In a large skillet, cook beef and onion over medium heat until meat is no longer pink; drain. Add the macaroni and cheese and salsa.

2. Transfer to a greased 1-qt. baking dish. Sprinkle with cheddar cheese. Bake, covered, at 350° for 25 minutes or until heated through.

1 serving: 393 cal., 19g fat (12g sat. fat), 74mg chol., 773mg sod., 27g carb. (8g sugars, 3g fiber), 24g pro.

SPICY BEEF BRISKET

SPICY BEEF BRISKET

My family fell in love with this brisket the first time I tried the recipe. The no-fuss preparation and long cooking time make it perfect to have simmering while you get ready for a party or holiday dinner.

—Mary Neihouse, Fort Smith, AR

Prep: 5 min. • **Bake:** 3 hours
Makes: 10 servings

- 1 fresh beef brisket (3 to 4 lbs.)
- 1 can (15 oz.) tomato sauce
- 1 can (10 oz.) diced tomatoes and green chiles, undrained
- 1 envelope onion soup mix
- ¼ tsp. garlic powder

Place brisket on a rack in a shallow greased roasting pan. In a small bowl, combine the remaining ingredients; pour over brisket. Cover and bake at 325° for 3 hours or until meat is tender. To serve, thinly slice across the grain.

4 oz. cooked beef: 195 cal., 6g fat (2g sat. fat), 58mg chol., 601mg sod., 5g carb. (1g sugars, 1g fiber), 29g pro. **Diabetic exchanges:** 4 lean meat.

SIZZLE & SMOKE FLAT IRON STEAKS

Smoked paprika and chipotle pepper give this version of blackened steak a spicy southwestern flair. To cool things off, add a salad of leafy greens with fruit and cheeses.
—Denise Pounds, Hutchinson, KS

Takes: 20 min.
Makes: 4 servings

- 1½ tsp. smoked paprika
- 1 tsp. salt
- 1 tsp. ground chipotle pepper
- ½ tsp. pepper
- 1¼ lbs. beef flat iron steaks or top sirloin steak (¾ in. thick)
- 2 Tbsp. butter
- Lime wedges, optional

1. Combine seasonings; rub over steaks. In a large skillet, cook beef in butter over medium-high heat for 30 seconds on each side. Reduce heat to medium; cook steaks for 5-7 minutes on each side or until meat reaches desired doneness (for medium-rare, a thermometer should read 135°; medium, 140°; medium-well, 145°).

2. Cut into slices; serve with lime wedges if desired.

3¾ oz cooked beef: 305 cal., 21g fat (10g sat. fat), 106mg chol., 725mg sod., 1g carb. (0 sugars, 1g fiber), 27g pro.

DIJON BEEF TENDERLOIN

DIJON BEEF TENDERLOIN

I like having an ace recipe up my sleeve, and this tenderloin with Dijon is my go-to for birthdays, buffets and holidays.
—Donna Lindecamp, Morganton, NC

Takes: 20 min.
Makes: 4 servings

- 4 beef tenderloin steaks (1 in. thick and 4 oz. each)
- ½ tsp. salt
- ¼ tsp. pepper
- 5 Tbsp. butter, divided
- 1 large onion, halved and thinly sliced
- 1 cup beef stock
- 1 Tbsp. Dijon mustard

1. Sprinkle tenderloin steaks with salt and pepper. In a large skillet, heat 2 Tbsp. butter over medium-high heat. Add the steaks; cook about 4-6 minutes on each side or until the meat reaches desired doneness (for medium-rare, a thermometer should read 135°; medium, 140°; medium-well, 145°). Remove steaks from pan; keep warm.
2. In same pan, heat 1 Tbsp. butter over medium heat. Add onion; cook and stir 4-6 minutes or until tender. Stir in stock; bring to a boil. Cook 1-2 minutes or until liquid is reduced by half. Stir in mustard; remove from heat. Cube remaining butter; stir into sauce just until blended. Serve with steaks.
3 oz. cooked beef with ¼ cup sauce: 317 cal., 21g fat (12g sat. fat), 88mg chol., 626mg sod., 5g carb. (2g sugars, 1g fiber), 26g pro.

SLOW-COOKED ONION MEAT LOAF

My husband and I really enjoy this delicious meat loaf. It's so simple to make with just five ingredients. Leftovers are good in sandwiches.
—Rhonda Cowden, Quincy, IL

Prep: 15 min. • **Cook:** 5 hours
Makes: 8 servings

- 2 large eggs, beaten
- ¾ cup quick-cooking oats
- ½ cup ketchup
- 1 envelope onion soup mix
- 2 lbs. ground beef

1. Cut three 20x3-in. strips of heavy-duty foil; crisscross so they resemble spokes of a wheel. Place strips on the bottom and up the side of a 3-qt. slow cooker. Coat strips with cooking spray.
2. In a large bowl, combine the eggs, oats, ketchup and soup mix. Crumble beef over mixture and mix lightly but thoroughly. Shape into a loaf. Place loaf in the center of the strips. Cover and cook on low for 5-6 hours or until a thermometer reads 160°.
3. Using foil strips as handles, remove meat loaf to a platter.
1 piece: 276 cal., 15g fat (6g sat. fat), 117mg chol., 579mg sod., 11g carb. (4g sugars, 1g fiber), 23g pro.

SLOW-COOKED
ONION MEAT LOAF

EASY & ELEGANT TENDERLOIN ROAST

I love the simplicity of the rub in this recipe—olive oil, garlic, salt and pepper. Just add it to the tenderloin and pop it in the oven for a perfect roast.

—Mary Kandell, Huron, OH

Prep: 10 min.
Bake: 45 min. + standing
Makes: 12 servings

- 1 beef tenderloin (5 lbs.)
- 2 Tbsp. olive oil
- 4 garlic cloves, minced
- 2 tsp. sea salt
- 1½ tsp. coarsely ground pepper

1. Preheat oven to 425°. Place beef tenderloin on a rack in a shallow roasting pan. In a small bowl, mix the olive oil, garlic, salt and pepper; rub over the roast.

2. Roast until the meat reaches desired doneness (for medium-rare, a thermometer should read 135°; medium, 140°; medium-well, 145°), 45-65 minutes. Remove roast from the oven; tent with foil. Let roast stand 15 minutes before slicing.

5 oz. cooked beef: 294 cal., 13g fat (5g sat. fat), 82mg chol., 394mg sod., 1g carb. (0 sugars, 0 fiber), 40g pro. **Diabetic exchanges:** 5 lean meat, ½ fat.

EASY & ELEGANT TENDERLOIN ROAST

VEGETABLE BEEF RAGOUT

Prepared beef tips and gravy can be found in the meat section of your grocery store. Add your favorite vegetables to this tasty convenience item for a quick and delicious meal.

—*Taste of Home* Test Kitchen

Takes: 20 min.
Makes: 4 servings

- 1 cup sliced fresh mushrooms
- ½ cup chopped onion
- 1 Tbsp. canola oil
- 1 pkg. (15 oz.) refrigerated beef tips with gravy
- 1 pkg. (14 oz.) frozen sugar snap peas, thawed
- 1 cup cherry tomatoes, halved
- Hot cooked pasta, optional

In a large skillet, saute the mushrooms and onion in oil until tender. Add the beef tips with gravy, peas and tomatoes; heat through. Serve over pasta if desired.

1 cup: 246 cal., 10g fat (3g sat. fat), 47mg chol., 670mg sod., 15g carb. (10g sugars, 4g fiber), 21g pro. **Diabetic exchanges:** 2 vegetable, 2 lean meat, ½ starch, ½ fat.

FIESTA RAVIOLI

FIESTA RAVIOLI

I adapted this recipe to suit our taste for spicy food. The ravioli taste like mini enchiladas. I serve them with a Mexican-inspired salad and pineapple sherbet for dessert.

—Debbie Purdue, Westland, MI

Takes: 20 min.
Makes: 6 servings

- 1 pkg. (25 oz.) frozen beef ravioli
- 1 can (10 oz.) enchilada sauce
- 1 cup salsa
- 2 cups shredded Monterey Jack cheese
- 1 can (2¼ oz.) sliced ripe olives, drained

1. Cook ravioli according to package directions. Meanwhile, in a large skillet, combine the enchilada sauce and salsa. Cook and stir over medium heat until heated through.

2. Drain ravioli; add to the sauce and gently stir to coat. Top with cheese and olives. Cover and cook over low heat until cheese is melted, 3-4 minutes.

1 serving: 470 cal., 20g fat (9g sat. fat), 74mg chol., 1342mg sod., 48g carb. (4g sugars, 6g fiber), 23g pro.

GOLOMBKI

GOLOMBKI

These cabbage rolls are stuffed with a delicious mixture of ground beef and onion. Instant rice and canned tomato soup speed along the prep work, and the long oven time gives you a chance to whip up a side dish and pour the wine.

—Valerie Lipinski, Buffalo, NY

Prep: 25 min. • **Bake:** 55 min.
Makes: 5 servings

- 1 medium head cabbage
- ½ cup uncooked instant rice
- 1 lb. ground beef
- 1 small onion, chopped
- ½ tsp. salt
- ¼ tsp. pepper
- 2 cans (10¾ oz. each) condensed tomato soup, undiluted
- 1¼ cups water

1. Cook the cabbage in boiling water just until outer leaves pull away easily from head. Set aside 10 large leaves for rolls. Refrigerate remaining cabbage for another use. Cut out the thick vein from the bottom of each leaf, making a V-shaped cut.
2. Cook rice according to package directions. Meanwhile, in a large skillet, cook beef and onion over medium heat until meat is no longer pink; drain. Stir in the cooked rice, salt and pepper.
3. Place ⅓ cup beef mixture on a cabbage leaf; overlap cut ends of leaf. Fold in sides. Beginning from the cut end, roll up. Repeat. Place seam side down in a greased 13x9-in. baking dish. Combine soup and water; pour over top.
4. Cover and bake at 350° for 55-65 minutes or until cabbage is tender.

2 cabbage rolls: 342 cal., 11g fat (4g sat. fat), 56mg chol., 1030mg sod., 40g carb. (18g sugars, 6g fiber), 21g pro.

SLOW-COOKED HOISIN POT ROAST

SLOW-COOKED HOISIN POT ROAST

One day my husband said that he loved plums and meat. The next time I put a roast in the slow cooker, I added some plums. He was onto something!
—Jacqueline Cole, Worthington, OH

Prep: 20 min. • **Cook:** 8 hours
Makes: 10 servings

- 1 medium onion, cut into 1-in. pieces
- 1 boneless beef chuck roast (4 to 5 lbs.)
- 1 Tbsp. canola oil
- 1 cup water
- 1 cup hoisin sauce
- 3 medium plums or 6 pitted dried plums (prunes), halved

Place onion in a 5-qt. slow cooker. Cut roast in half. In a large skillet, heat oil over medium-high heat; brown meat. Transfer meat to slow cooker. Combine water and hoisin sauce; pour over meat. Top with plums. Cook, covered, on low until meat is tender, 8-10 hours. If desired, skim fat.

7 oz. cooked meat with ¼ cup sauce:: 389 cal., 20g fat (7g sat. fat), 119mg chol., 488mg sod., 15g carb. (9g sugars, 1g fiber), 37g pro.

BASIL-BUTTER STEAKS WITH ROASTED POTATOES

BASIL-BUTTER STEAKS WITH ROASTED POTATOES

A few items and 30 minutes are all you'll need for this incredibly satisfying meal. A simple basil butter gives these steaks a very special taste.

—Taste of Home Test Kitchen

Takes: 30 min.
Makes: 4 servings

- 1 pkg. (15 oz.) frozen Parmesan and roasted garlic red potato wedges
- 4 beef tenderloin steaks (1¼ in. thick and 6 oz. each)
- ½ tsp. salt
- ½ tsp. pepper
- 5 Tbsp. butter, divided
- 2 cups grape tomatoes
- 1 Tbsp. minced fresh basil

1. Bake potato wedges according to package directions.
2. Meanwhile, sprinkle steaks with salt and pepper. In a 10-in. cast-iron or other ovenproof skillet, brown steaks in 2 Tbsp. butter. Add tomatoes to skillet. Bake, uncovered, at 425° until meat reaches desired doneness, 15-20 minutes (for medium-rare, a thermometer should read 135°; medium, 140°; medium-well, 145°).
3. In a small bowl, combine basil and remaining butter. Spoon over steaks, and serve steaks with potatoes.

1 serving: 538 cal., 29g fat (13g sat. fat), 112mg chol., 740mg sod., 27g carb. (2g sugars, 3g fiber), 41g pro.

BIG BRISKET BURGERS

BIG BRISKET BURGERS

Take one all-American patty and load it up Texas-style with brisket on Texas toast.

—Taste of Home Test Kitchen

Takes: 25 min.
Makes: 4 servings

- ½ cup seasoned bread crumbs
- 1 large egg, lightly beaten
- ½ tsp. salt
- ½ tsp. pepper
- 1 lb. ground beef
- 1 Tbsp. olive oil
- 8 slices Texas toast, toasted
- Barbecued brisket, sliced and warmed

1. In a large bowl, combine bread crumbs, egg, salt and pepper. Add the ground beef; mix lightly but thoroughly. Shape into four ½-in.-thick patties. Press a shallow indentation in the center of each with your thumb. Brush both sides of patties with oil.
2. Grill burgers, covered, over medium heat or broil 4 in. from heat 4-5 minutes on each side or until a thermometer reads 160°. Serve between Texas toast, topped with brisket.

1 burger: 402 cal., 20g fat (6g sat. fat), 117mg chol., 769mg sod., 27g carb. (2g sugars, 2g fiber), 27g pro.

GARLIC-BUTTER STEAK

GARLIC-BUTTER STEAK

This quick and easy skillet entree is definitely restaurant quality and sure to become a staple at your house, too!
—Lily Julow, Lawrenceville, GA

Takes: 20 min.
Makes: 2 servings

- 2 Tbsp. butter, softened, divided
- 1 tsp. minced fresh parsley
- ½ tsp. minced garlic
- ¼ tsp. reduced-sodium soy sauce
- 1 beef flat iron steak or boneless top sirloin steak (¾ lb.)
- ⅛ tsp. salt
- ⅛ tsp. pepper

1. Mix 1 Tbsp. butter with parsley, garlic and soy sauce.
2. Sprinkle steak with salt and pepper. In a large skillet, heat remaining butter over medium heat. Add steak; cook until meat reaches desired doneness (for medium-rare, a thermometer should read 135°; medium, 140°; medium-well, 145°), 4-7 minutes per side. Serve steak with the garlic butter.

4 oz. cooked beef with 2 tsp. garlic butter: 316 cal., 20g fat (10g sat. fat), 124mg chol., 337mg sod., 0 carb. (0 sugars, 0 fiber), 32g pro.

TEST KITCHEN TIP
To keep your steak juicy and tender, you want an even sear and seal. You can best accomplish this by not moving or turning the meat until halfway through cooking time.

BEEF BRISKET TACOS

Birthday parties back home were big gatherings of cousins, aunts, uncles, grandparents and anyone else we considered family. As soon as guests arrived, hot pans of shredded brisket, or carne deshebrada, *appeared, along with huge bowls of salads,* frijoles, *tostadas and salsas. Brisket was the dish we counted on because it could be made in the oven or a slow cooker.*

—Yvette Marquez, Littleton, CO

Prep: 15 min. + marinating
Cook: 8 hours
Makes: 10 servings

- 1 bottle (12 oz.) beer or nonalcoholic beer
- 1 cup brisket marinade sauce or liquid smoke plus 1 Tbsp. salt
- 2 bay leaves
- ½ tsp. salt
- ½ tsp. pepper
- 1 fresh beef brisket (3 to 4 lbs.), fat trimmed
- 20 corn tortillas (6 in.), warmed
- Optional: Shredded cheddar cheese, lime wedges, media crema table cream, fresh cilantro leaves, thinly sliced green onions, jalapeno slices and salsa

1. In a small bowl or shallow dish, combine the beer, sauce, bay leaves, salt and pepper. Add brisket; turn to coat. Cover and refrigerate brisket overnight.

2. Transfer brisket and marinade to a 6-qt. slow cooker. Cook, covered, on low 8-10 hours or until tender. Remove meat; discard bay leaves. Reserve juices in slow cooker. When cool enough to handle, shred meat with 2 forks. Return to slow cooker.

3. Using tongs, serve shredded brisket in tortillas. Add toppings as desired.

Freeze option: Freeze cooled meat mixture and juices in freezer containers. To use, partially thaw in refrigerator overnight. Heat through in a saucepan, stirring occasionally.

Note: This is a fresh beef brisket, not corned beef. This recipe was tested with Claude's Barbeque Brisket Marinade Sauce.

2 tacos: 278 cal., 7g fat (2g sat. fat), 58mg chol., 947mg sod., 21g carb. (0 sugars, 3g fiber), 31g pro.

BEEF BRISKET TACOS

★★★★★ **READER REVIEW**

"These were terrific! I didn't change a thing. Definitely going to make this one again!"

—TAMMY BRACKLEY, TASTEOFHOME.COM

SIZZLING ANCHO RIBEYES

In our house, we love the taste of chipotle peppers on just about anything. This delicious recipe proves that there might not be a better pairing than chipotle and grilled steak.
—Angela Spengler, Niceville, FL

Takes: 25 min.
Makes: 6 servings

- 4 tsp. salt
- 4 tsp. ground ancho chile pepper
- 1 tsp. pepper
- 6 beef ribeye steaks (¾ lb. each)
- 6 Tbsp. butter, softened
- 6 chipotle peppers in adobo sauce

1. In a small bowl, combine the salt, chile pepper and pepper; rub over steaks. In another small bowl, beat butter and chipotle peppers until blended.
2. Grill steaks, covered, over medium heat or broil 4 in. from the heat for 5-7 minutes on each side or until meat reaches desired doneness (for medium-rare, a thermometer should read 135°; medium, 140°; medium-well, 145°). Serve with the chipotle butter.
1 steak with about 1 Tbsp. butter: 867 cal., 66g fat (29g sat. fat), 232mg chol., 1926mg sod., 2g carb. (1g sugars, 1g fiber), 61g pro.

SMASH BURGERS

Now's not the time to skimp on salt or cut calories. Go for ground chuck if you can. If you can find a blend with ground brisket or short rib, all the better. The best burger comes with kosher salt—it's beef's best friend.

—James Schend,
Pleasant Prairie, WI

Takes: 15 min.
Makes: 4 servings

- 1 lb. ground beef (preferably 80% lean)
- 1 tsp. canola oil
- 1 tsp. kosher salt, divided
- 1 tsp. coarsely ground pepper, divided
- 4 hamburger buns, split
- Optional: Mayonnaise, sliced American cheese, sliced tomato, dill pickle slices, lettuce, ketchup and yellow mustard

1. Place a 9-in. cast-iron skillet over medium heat. Meanwhile, gently shape beef into 4 balls, shaping just enough to keep together (do not compact).
2. Increase burner temperature to medium-high; add oil. Working in batches, add the beef. With a heavy metal spatula, flatten to ¼- to ½-in. thickness; sprinkle each with ⅛ tsp. salt and pepper. Cook until edges start to brown, about 1½ minutes. Turn the burgers and sprinkle each with additional ⅛ tsp. salt and pepper. Cook until well browned and a thermometer reads at least 160°, about 1 minute. Repeat with remaining beef.
3. Serve burgers on buns with toppings as desired.

1 burger: 339 cal., 16g fat (5g sat. fat), 70mg chol., 760mg sod., 22g carb. (3g sugars, 1g fiber), 24g pro.

TEST KITCHEN TIP
After you "smash" or flatten the burgers, don't move them until ready to flip. Flip the burger onto an unused area of the skillet; it's much hotter than the section of pan where the burger was.

BLUE CHEESE-
STUFFED STEAKS

BLUE CHEESE-STUFFED STEAKS

For a fast, fancy dinner, try this tender beef with a mild blue cheese stuffing. Grape tomatoes sauteed in garlic make a colorful and flavorful accompaniment.
—Teddy Devico, Warren, NJ

Takes: 30 min.
Makes: 4 servings

- 10 garlic cloves, peeled
- 2 Tbsp. canola oil
- 4 cups grape tomatoes
- 4 boneless beef top loin steaks (8 oz. each)
- ½ cup crumbled blue cheese
- ½ tsp. salt
- ¼ tsp. pepper

1. In a large skillet, saute garlic in oil until tender. Cover and cook over low heat for 5-7 minutes or until golden and softened. Add tomatoes; cook and stir until tomatoes just begin to burst. Remove from the skillet; set aside and keep warm.
2. Cut a pocket in the thickest part of each steak; fill with the blue cheese. Sprinkle with salt and pepper.
3. In the same skillet, cook the steaks over medium heat for 4-5 minutes on each side or until the meat reaches desired doneness (for medium-rare, a thermometer should read 135°; medium, 140°; medium-well, 145°). Serve steaks with the tomato mixture.

1 steak with 1 cup tomato mixture: 463 cal., 23g fat (8g sat. fat), 113mg chol., 644mg sod., 10g carb. (4g sugars, 2g fiber), 53g pro.

CHOCOLATE-CHIPOTLE SIRLOIN STEAK

Looking to do something a little different with grilled sirloin? Add smoky heat and chocolaty rich color with this easy five-ingredient rub.
—*Taste of Home* Test Kitchen

Prep: 10 min. + chilling
Grill: 20 min. • **Makes:** 4 servings

- 3 Tbsp. baking cocoa
- 2 Tbsp. chopped chipotle peppers in adobo sauce
- 4 tsp. Worcestershire sauce
- 2 tsp. brown sugar
- ½ tsp. salt
- 1½ lbs. beef top sirloin steak

1. Place the first 5 ingredients in a blender; cover and process until blended. Rub over the beef. Cover and refrigerate for at least 2 hours.
2. Grill the beef, covered, over medium heat or broil 4 in. from heat for 8-10 minutes on each side or until meat reaches desired doneness (for medium-rare, a thermometer should read 135°; medium, 140°; medium-well, 145°).

5 oz. cooked beef: 246 cal., 7g fat (3g sat. fat), 69mg chol., 477mg sod., 6g carb. (3g sugars, 1g fiber), 37g pro. **Diabetic exchanges:** 5 lean meat.

CHOCOLATE-CHIPOTLE
SIRLOIN STEAK

PRESTO BEEF STEW

This quick, flavorful dinner for two couldn't be easier. Just combine sauteed mushrooms with shredded beef, then serve with golden-brown biscuits. Sometimes I add sliced green onions to the stew.

—Karla Johnson, East Helena, MT

Takes: 30 min.
Makes: 2 servings

- 2 individually frozen biscuits
- 2 Tbsp. butter
- 2 cups sliced fresh mushrooms
- 1 pkg. (17 oz.) refrigerated beef roast au jus
- ¼ tsp. pepper
- 2 Tbsp. cornstarch
- 1 cup cold water

1. Bake biscuits according to package directions.
2. Meanwhile, in a large saucepan over medium heat, melt butter. Add mushrooms; cook and stir until tender. Shred beef with 2 forks; add to the pan. Add pepper. Combine cornstarch and water until smooth; stir into stew. Bring to a boil; cook and stir for 1-2 minutes or until thickened.
3. Divide stew between 2 bowls; top each with a biscuit.

1 serving: 710 cal., 40g fat (18g sat. fat), 176mg chol., 1595mg sod., 38g carb. (10g sugars, 2g fiber), 54g pro.

SALT-ENCRUSTED RIB ROAST

A rib roast is a big part of our holiday dinner traditions. We love the yellow mustard, but you can use your favorite—Dijon and others are fair game.

—Rebecca Wirtzberger, Yuma, AZ

Prep: 15 min.
Bake: 2½ hours + standing
Makes: 10 servings

- 1 bone-in beef rib roast (about 6 lbs.)
- ½ cup yellow mustard
- 3 cups kosher salt (about 1½ lbs.)
- ½ cup water

1. Preheat oven to 450°. Place rib roast in a roasting pan, fat side up; spread all sides with the mustard. In a bowl, mix salt and water to make a dry paste (mixture should be just moist enough to pack); press onto top and sides of roast.
2. Roast 15 minutes. Reduce oven setting to 325°. Roast 2¼-2¾ hours longer or until a thermometer inserted in beef reaches 135° for medium-rare; 140° for medium; 145° for medium-well. (Temperature of roast will continue to rise about 10° upon standing.) Let stand 20 minutes before serving.
3. Remove and discard salt crust. Carve roast into slices.

5 oz. cooked beef: 320 cal., 18g fat (7g sat. fat), 0 chol., 997mg sod., 1g carb. (0 sugars, 0 fiber), 37g pro.

SALT-ENCRUSTED RIB ROAST

GRILLED RIBEYE WITH GARLIC BLUE CHEESE MUSTARD SAUCE

GRILLED RIBEYE WITH GARLIC BLUE CHEESE MUSTARD SAUCE

This simple steak gets a big flavor boost from two of my favorites: mustard and blue cheese. We make this to celebrate our anniversary!
—Ashley Lecker, Green Bay, WI

Prep: 20 min.
Grill: 10 min. + standing
Makes: 4 servings

- 1 cup half-and-half cream
- ½ cup Dijon mustard
- ¼ cup plus 2 tsp. crumbled blue cheese, divided
- 1 garlic clove, minced
- 2 beef ribeye steaks (1½ in. thick and 12 oz. each)
- 1 Tbsp. olive oil
- ¼ tsp. salt
- ¼ tsp. pepper

1. In a small saucepan over medium heat, whisk together cream, mustard, ¼ cup blue cheese and garlic. Bring to a simmer. Reduce heat to low; whisk occasionally.

2. Meanwhile, rub meat with olive oil; sprinkle with salt and pepper. Grill steaks, covered, on a greased rack over high direct heat 4-6 minutes on each side until meat reaches desired doneness (for medium-rare, a thermometer should read 135°; medium, 140°; medium-well, 145°). Remove from grill; let stand 10 minutes while sauce finishes cooking. When the sauce is reduced by half, pour over steaks; top with remaining 2 tsp. blue cheese.

½ steak with 3 Tbsp. sauce: 547 cal., 39g fat (17g sat. fat), 138mg chol., 1088mg sod., 3g carb. (2g sugars, 0 fiber), 34g pro.

★★★★★ READER REVIEW
"Wonderful sauce. Just the right amount of mustard flavor. We've used it on steaks, burgers and grilled pork chops."
—REBELWITHOUTACLUE, TASTEOFHOME.COM

FLANK STEAK WITH CILANTRO SALSA VERDE

FLANK STEAK WITH CILANTRO SALSA VERDE

Steak is always a winner in our house. To make it extra special, I add jarred salsa verde and top with freshly chopped tomato and avocado. It's a colorful and delicious combination!

—Lily Julow, Lawrenceville, GA

Takes: 25 min.
Makes: 4 servings

- 1 beef flank steak or top sirloin steak, 1 in. thick (about 1¼ lbs.)
- ¼ tsp. salt
- ¼ tsp. pepper
- 1 cup salsa verde
- ½ cup fresh cilantro leaves
- 1 medium ripe avocado, peeled and diced
- 1 medium tomato, seeded and diced

1. Sprinkle the steak with salt and pepper. Grill steak, covered, over medium heat or broil 4 in. from heat 6-9 minutes per side or until meat reaches desired doneness (for medium-rare, a thermometer should read 135°; medium, 140°; medium-well, 145°). Let stand 5 minutes.

2. Meanwhile, process the salsa and cilantro in a food processor until blended. Slice the steak thinly across the grain; serve with the salsa mixture, avocado and tomato.

1 serving: 263 cal., 15g fat (4g sat. fat), 54mg chol., 571mg sod., 8g carb. (2g sugars, 4g fiber), 24g pro. **Diabetic exchanges:** 3 lean meat, 2 fat.

GRILLED ITALIAN BURGERS

While trying to think of a new way to fix hamburgers with the same old ground beef, I came up with an Italian twist. They're perfect with a side salad or fresh green beans.

—Rebekah Beyer, Sabetha, KS

Takes: 20 min.
Makes: 4 servings

- 1 cup shredded part-skim mozzarella cheese, divided
- 1 tsp. Worcestershire sauce
- ¼ tsp. Italian seasoning
- ⅛ tsp. salt
- ⅛ tsp. pepper
- 1 lb. ground beef
- Marinara or spaghetti sauce, warmed

1. In a large bowl, combine ½ cup cheese, Worcestershire sauce and seasonings. Add beef; mix lightly but thoroughly. Shape into four ½-in.-thick patties.

2. Grill burgers, covered, over medium heat or broil 4 in. from heat until a thermometer reads 160°, 4-5 minutes on each side. Sprinkle with remaining cheese; grill, covered, until cheese is melted, 1-2 minutes longer. Serve with marinara sauce.

1 burger: 279 cal., 18g fat (8g sat. fat), 86mg chol., 282mg sod., 1g carb. (1g sugars, 0 fiber), 27g pro.

GRILLED ITALIAN BURGERS

BALSAMIC-GLAZED
BEEF SKEWERS

BEEF BRISKET MARINARA

BALSAMIC-GLAZED BEEF SKEWERS

With only simple ingredients, these mouthwatering kabobs are a summertime favorite. To prevent wooden skewers from burning, soak them in water for 30 minutes before threading on the meat and tomatoes.
—Carole Fraser, Toronto, ON

Takes: 25 min.
Makes: 4 servings

- ¼ cup balsamic vinaigrette
- ¼ cup barbecue sauce
- 1 tsp. Dijon mustard
- 1 lb. beef top sirloin steak, cut into 1-in. cubes
- 2 cups cherry tomatoes

1. In a large bowl, whisk the vinaigrette, barbecue sauce and mustard until blended. Reserve ¼ cup mixture for basting. Add beef to remaining mixture; toss to coat.
2. Alternately thread the beef and cherry tomatoes on 4 metal or soaked wooden skewers. Lightly grease grill rack.
3. Grill skewers, covered, over medium heat or broil 4 in. from heat 6-9 minutes or until beef reaches desired doneness, turning occasionally and basting frequently with the reserved vinaigrette mixture during the last 3 minutes.
1 skewer: 194 cal., 7g fat (2g sat. fat), 46mg chol., 288mg sod., 7g carb. (5g sugars, 1g fiber), 25g pro. **Diabetic exchanges:** 3 lean meat, 1½ fat, ½ starch.

BEEF BRISKET MARINARA

Marinara sauce and tender meat are real comfort food, especially when served with mashed potatoes, rice or pasta.
—Donna-Marie Ryan, Topsfield, MA

Prep: 10 min. • **Cook:** 3¾ hours
Makes: 10 servings

- 1 fresh beef brisket (4 lbs.)
- ½ tsp. salt
- ¼ tsp. pepper
- 2 Tbsp. olive oil
- 2 celery ribs, finely chopped
- 1 medium carrot, finely chopped
- ½ cup dry red wine or beef broth
- 1 jar (24 oz.) marinara sauce

1. Sprinkle brisket with salt and pepper. In a Dutch oven, heat oil over medium heat. Brown the brisket on both sides. Remove from pan.
2. Add the celery and carrot to same pan; cook and stir until crisp-tender, 2-3 minutes. Add the wine; cook, stirring to loosen browned bits from pan. Stir in the marinara sauce.
3. Return brisket to pan; bring to a boil. Reduce heat; simmer, covered, 3½-4 hours or until meat is tender.
4. Remove brisket from pan. Skim fat from sauce. Cut brisket diagonally across the grain into thin slices; serve with sauce.
5 oz. cooked beef with ½ cup sauce: 295 cal., 11g fat (3g sat. fat), 77mg chol., 307mg sod., 9g carb. (6g sugars, 1g fiber), 38g pro. **Diabetic exchanges:** 5 lean meat, ½ starch, ½ fat.

POULTRY GREATS

GLAZED ROAST CHICKEN
P. 85

1

2

3

4

5

WHEN IT COMES TO FAST, FLAVORFUL DINNERS, CHICKEN AND TURKEY ARE NATURAL CHOICES!

CHICKEN WITH CHERRY WINE SAUCE

CHICKEN WITH CHERRY WINE SAUCE

My dad's a chef, and I learned to cook at an early age. This saucy chicken was the first dish I made by myself, and I still enjoy it to this day.

—Ben Diaz, Azusa, CA

Takes: 30 min.
Makes: 4 servings

- 4 boneless skinless chicken breast halves (8 oz. each)
- ¼ tsp. salt
- ¼ tsp. pepper
- 7 Tbsp. butter, divided
- ⅔ cup dry red wine
- 1 Tbsp. sugar
- ½ cup fresh or frozen pitted dark sweet cherries, thawed

1. Preheat oven to 350°. Sprinkle chicken with salt and pepper. In a large cast-iron or other ovenproof skillet, heat 2 Tbsp. butter over medium-high heat. Brown chicken on both sides. Bake until a thermometer reads 165°, 12-15 minutes.

2. Meanwhile, in a small saucepan, combine wine and sugar. Bring to a boil; cook, uncovered, until liquid is reduced by half, 4-5 minutes. Reduce heat to low; whisk in remaining butter, 1 Tbsp. at a time, until blended. Stir in cherries; serve with chicken.

1 chicken breast half with 3 Tbsp. sauce: 480 cal., 25g fat (14g sat. fat), 179mg chol., 418mg sod., 8g carb. (5g sugars, 0 fiber), 46g pro.

Pork Chops with Cherry Wine Sauce: Substitute 6 bone-in pork loin chops (8 oz. each) for chicken breasts. Proceed as directed, increasing bake time to 25-30 minutes or until a thermometer reads 145°. Let stand 5 minutes before serving.

APPLE-GLAZED CHICKEN THIGHS

APPLE-GLAZED CHICKEN THIGHS

My child is choosy but willing to eat this chicken glazed with apple juice. I dish it up with mashed potatoes.

—Kerry Picard, Spokane, WA

Takes: 25 min.
Makes: 6 servings

- 6 boneless skinless chicken thighs (1½ lbs.)
- ¾ tsp. seasoned salt
- ¼ tsp. pepper
- 1 Tbsp. canola oil
- 1 cup unsweetened apple juice
- 1 tsp. minced fresh thyme or ¼ tsp. dried thyme

1. Sprinkle chicken with seasoned salt and pepper. In a large skillet, heat oil over medium-high heat. Brown chicken on both sides. Remove from pan.

2. Add juice and thyme to skillet. Bring to a boil, stirring to loosen browned bits from pan; cook until liquid is reduced by half. Return chicken to pan; cook, covered, over medium heat 3-4 minutes longer or until a thermometer inserted in chicken reads 170°.

1 chicken thigh with about 1 Tbsp. glaze: 204 cal., 11g fat (2g sat. fat), 76mg chol., 255mg sod., 5g carb. (4g sugars, 0 fiber), 21g pro. **Diabetic exchanges:** 3 lean meat, ½ fat.

PRESSURE-COOKER LEMON CHICKEN WITH BASIL

No matter when I eat it, this tangy chicken dish always reminds me of summer meals. The recipe produces a lot of lovely sauce; spoon it over some herbed couscous or simply serve it as is.
—Deborah Posey, Virgina Beach, VA

Takes: 20 minutes
Makes: 4 servings

- 4 boneless skinless chicken breast halves (6 oz. each)
- 2 medium lemons
- 1 bunch fresh basil leaves (¾ oz.)
- 2 cups chicken stock

1. Place chicken in a 6-qt. electric pressure cooker. Finely grate enough zest from lemons to measure 4 tsp. Cut lemons in half; squeeze juice. Add zest and juice to pressure cooker.
2. Tear the basil leaves directly into pressure cooker; add the chicken stock. Lock lid; close pressure-release valve. Adjust to pressure-cook on high for 6 minutes. Quick-release pressure. A thermometer inserted in chicken should read at least 165°. When cool enough to handle, shred the meat with 2 forks; return to pressure cooker. If desired, stir in additional lemon zest and chopped basil. Serve with a slotted spoon.
Freeze option: Place the chicken and cooking liquid in freezer containers. Cool and freeze. To use, partially thaw in refrigerator overnight. Microwave, covered, on high in a microwave-safe dish until heated through, stirring gently.
5 oz. cooked chicken: 200 cal., 4g fat (1g sat. fat), 94mg chol., 337mg sod., 3g carb. (1g sugars, 0 fiber), 37g pro. **Diabetic exchanges:** 5 lean meat.

PRESSURE-COOKER LEMON CHICKEN WITH BASIL

CHIP-CRUSTED CHICKEN

Dijon-mayo and barbecue potato chips might sound strange together, but the flavors combine beautifully in this entree.
—Mike Tchou, Pepper Pike, OH

Takes: 30 min.
Makes: 6 servings

- ⅔ cup Dijon-mayonnaise blend
- 6 cups barbecue potato chips, finely crushed
- 6 boneless skinless chicken breast halves (5 oz. each)

1. Place the mayonnaise blend and potato chips in separate shallow bowls. Dip chicken in mayonnaise blend, then coat with chips.
2. Place on an ungreased baking sheet. Bake chicken at 375° until a thermometer reads 165°, 20-25 minutes.
1 serving: 397 cal., 16g fat (5g sat. fat), 78mg chol., 1015mg sod., 29g carb. (1g sugars, 1g fiber), 30g pro.

EASY BREEZY TURKEY LOAF

If you think you can't make meat loaf the way Mom does, try this easy recipe. Your favorite store-bought pasta sauce flavors the loaf, and the turkey saves on calories.
—Jo Ann Shappard, Vincennes, IN

Prep: 10 min. • **Bake:** 65 min.
Makes: 6 servings

- 1 cup seasoned bread crumbs
- 1 cup garden-style pasta sauce, divided
- 1 medium onion, chopped
- 1 large egg
- 1 tsp. salt
- 1 tsp. pepper
- 1½ lbs. ground turkey

1. In a large bowl, combine the bread crumbs, ½ cup pasta sauce, onion, egg, salt and pepper. Crumble turkey over mixture and mix lightly but thoroughly. Pat into an ungreased 9x5-in. loaf pan.
2. Bake, uncovered, at 350° for 1 hour. Spread remaining pasta sauce over loaf. Bake the loaf 5-10 minutes longer or until a thermometer reads 165° and the juices run clear.

Freeze option Securely wrap individual portions of cooled meat loaf in foil. To use, partially thaw in refrigerator overnight. Unwrap meat loaf; reheat on a greased shallow baking pan in a preheated 350° oven until heated through and a thermometer inserted in center reads 165°.
1 piece: 354 cal., 20g fat (6g sat. fat), 114mg chol., 973mg sod., 22g carb. (6g sugars, 2g fiber), 23g pro.

GORGONZOLA & ORANGE CHICKEN TENDERS

GORGONZOLA & ORANGE CHICKEN TENDERS

My mom likes to make this for family gatherings, and we all like to eat it. Marmalade and Gorgonzola might sound like an unusual combo, but they actually make a marvelous pair. Give it a try!

—Yvette Gorman, Denver, PA

Takes: 25 min.
Makes: 4 servings

- 1 large egg
- ¼ tsp. salt
- ¾ cup seasoned bread crumbs
- 1 lb. chicken tenderloins
- 2 Tbsp. olive oil
- ¼ cup orange marmalade, warmed
- ¼ cup crumbled Gorgonzola cheese

1. In a bowl, whisk egg and salt. Place bread crumbs in another shallow bowl. Dip the chicken in egg, then in bread crumbs, patting to help coating adhere.

2. In a large skillet, heat oil over medium heat. Add chicken; cook 3-4 minutes on each side or until chicken is no longer pink. Drizzle with warm marmalade; top with cheese. Remove from heat; let stand, covered, until cheese begins to melt.

1 serving: 318 cal., 12g fat (3g sat. fat), 108mg chol., 543mg sod., 23g carb. (13g sugars, 1g fiber), 32g pro.

HONEY THYME GRILLED CHICKEN

For grilling chicken, I wanted a marinade different from barbecue sauce, so I pulled out some honey and thyme. If you have time, let the chicken marinate awhile to boost flavor.

—Noel Bigelow, Alexandria, VA

Takes: 25 min.
Makes: 4 servings

- ¼ cup olive oil
- ¼ cup honey
- 1 garlic clove, minced
- 8 chicken drumsticks (about 2 lbs.)
- 1 tsp. dried thyme
- ¾ tsp. salt
- ¼ tsp. pepper

1. In a small bowl, whisk oil, honey and garlic until blended. Sprinkle the drumsticks with all seasonings.

2. Lightly oil grill rack with cooking oil. Grill the chicken, covered, over medium heat 15-20 minutes or until a thermometer reads 170°-175°, turning occasionally and brushing generously with the honey mixture during the last 5 minutes.

2 chicken drumsticks: 418 cal., 26g fat (5g sat. fat), 95mg chol., 531mg sod., 18g carb. (17g sugars, 0 fiber), 29g pro.

HONEY THYME GRILLED CHICKEN

FAVORITE LASAGNA ROLL-UPS

FAVORITE LASAGNA ROLL-UPS

This crowd-pleasing take on lasagna offers a new way to enjoy a classic dish in individual portions. And it requires only a few ingredients.

—Susan Sabia, Windsor, CA

Prep: 25 min. • **Bake:** 30 min.
Makes: 10 servings

- 10 uncooked lasagna noodles
- 1 pkg. (19½ oz.) Italian turkey sausage links, casings removed
- 1 pkg. (8 oz.) cream cheese, softened
- 1 jar (26 oz.) pasta sauce
- 1¾ cups shredded cheddar cheese, divided
- Minced fresh parsley, optional

1. Preheat oven to 350°. Cook noodles according to package directions. Meanwhile, in a large skillet, cook Italian sausage over medium heat until no longer pink, breaking it into crumbles; drain. Stir in cream cheese and ⅓ cup pasta sauce.
2. Drain noodles; spread ¼ cup meat mixture on each noodle. Sprinkle each with 2 Tbsp. cheese; carefully roll up.
3. Spread ⅔ cup pasta sauce into an ungreased 13x9-in. baking dish. Place roll-ups seam side down over sauce. Top with remaining sauce and cheese. Cover and bake for 20 minutes. Uncover; bake until sauce is bubbly, 10-15 minutes longer. If desired, sprinkle with parsley.

1 roll-up: 372 cal., 22g fat (11g sat. fat), 81mg chol., 885mg sod., 25g carb. (6g sugars, 2g fiber), 19g pro.

AIR-FRYER LEMON FETA CHICKEN

AIR-FRYER LEMON FETA CHICKEN

This bright, Greek-inspired chicken has only a few ingredients, making it a busy-day lifesaver! And popping it into the air fryer makes it even easier.

—Ann Cain, Morrill, NE

Takes: 25 min.
Makes: 2 servings

- 2 boneless skinless chicken breast halves (2 oz. each)
- 1 to 2 Tbsp. lemon juice
- 2 Tbsp. crumbled feta cheese
- ½ tsp. dried oregano
- ¼ tsp. pepper

1. Preheat air fryer to 400°. Place chicken in a lightly greased baking dish that fits into the air fryer. Pour lemon juice over chicken; sprinkle with feta cheese, oregano and pepper.
2. Cook until a thermometer reads 165°, 20-25 minutes.

1 chicken breast half: 142 cal., 4g fat (2g sat. fat), 66mg chol., 122mg sod., 1g carb. (0 sugars, 0 fiber), 24g pro.

SHREDDED CHICKEN TOSTADAS

These flavorful tostadas are super easy and family-friendly. You won't believe how tender and juicy the chicken comes out. Just load up the tostadas with your favorite toppings, and you have a simple meal.

—Lisa Kenny, Houston, TX

Prep: 10 min.
Cook: 8 minutes + releasing
Makes: 8 servings

- 2½ lbs. boneless skinless chicken breasts
- 1 envelope reduced-sodium taco seasoning
- 1 can (10 oz.) diced tomatoes and green chiles, undrained
- ½ tsp. salt
- 16 tostada shells
- 2 cups shredded Mexican cheese blend
- Optional: Shredded lettuce, chopped tomatoes, sliced avocado, sour cream, sliced jalapenos and fresh cilantro

1. Place chicken in a 3- or 4-qt. slow cooker. Sprinkle with the taco seasoning; top with diced tomatoes and green chiles. Cook chicken, covered, on low until a thermometer inserted into chicken reads 165°, 3-4 hours.

2. Shred meat with 2 forks. Return to slow cooker and add salt; heat through. Serve on tostada shells with cheese and optional ingredients as desired.

Pressure cooker option: Place ½ cup water in a 6-qt. electric pressure cooker. Add the chicken and sprinkle with taco seasoning. Top with diced tomatoes and green chiles. Lock lid; close pressure-release valve. Adjust to pressure cook on high for 8 minutes. Let pressure release naturally for 10 minutes; quick-release any remaining pressure. A thermometer inserted into chicken should read at least 165°. Shred meat with 2 forks. Return to pressure cooker and add the salt; heat through. Serve on tostada shells with cheese and optional toppings as desired.

Freeze option: Freeze cooled meat mixture and juices in freezer containers. To use, partially thaw in refrigerator overnight. Heat through in a saucepan, stirring occasionally; add a little water if necessary.

2 tostadas: 378 cal., 17g fat (7g sat. fat), 103mg chol., 858mg sod., 18g carb. (1g sugars, 1g fiber), 36g pro.

SHREDDED CHICKEN TOSTADAS

GLAZED ROAST CHICKEN

A few pantry items inspired this recipe, which I've since made for small weeknight meals and large weekend parties alike. The quince jelly always comes from my boss, who grows the fruit in his very own backyard.

—Victoria Miller, San Ramon, CA

Prep: 15 min.
Bake: 1½ hours + standing
Makes: 6 servings

- 1 cup white wine or chicken broth
- 1 cup apricot preserves or quince jelly
- 1 Tbsp. stone-ground mustard
- 1 broiler/fryer chicken (3 to 4 lbs.)
- ¾ tsp. salt
- ½ tsp. pepper

1. Preheat oven to 375°. In a small saucepan, bring wine to a boil; cook until wine is reduced by half, 3-4 minutes. Stir in the preserves and mustard. Reserve half of the glaze for serving.

2. Place chicken on a rack in a shallow roasting pan, breast side up. Sprinkle with salt and pepper. Tuck the wings under chicken; tie drumsticks together.

3. Roast 45 minutes; baste with glaze. Continue roasting chicken until a thermometer inserted in thigh reads 170°-175°, basting occasionally with glaze. Cover loosely with foil if the chicken browns too quickly. Remove chicken from oven; tent with foil. Let stand 15 minutes before carving. Serve with remaining reserved glaze.

1 serving: 437 cal., 17g fat (5g sat. fat), 104mg chol., 458mg sod., 35g carb. (23g sugars, 0 fiber), 34g pro.

TURKEY TENDERLOINS WITH SHALLOT BERRY SAUCE

The original recipe called for chicken and apricot, but I tried turkey and berry jam to use up some leftovers. It seems like a lot of ingredients, but there are really only a few.

—Kendra Doss,
Colorado Springs, CO

Prep: 15 min. • **Cook:** 25 min.
Makes: 8 servings

- 4 turkey breast tenderloins (12 oz. each)
- ½ tsp. salt
- ½ tsp. pepper
- 1 Tbsp. olive oil
- ¼ cup chicken broth

SAUCE

- 1 Tbsp. olive oil
- 5 shallots, thinly sliced
- ¼ tsp. salt
- ¼ tsp. pepper
- ½ cup chicken broth
- ¼ cup balsamic vinegar
- 3 Tbsp. seedless raspberry jam

1. Sprinkle the turkey with salt and pepper. In a large skillet, heat oil over medium heat; brown turkey tenderloins in batches. Cook, covered, until a thermometer inserted in center reads 165°, 8-10 minutes longer. Remove from pan; keep warm.

2. Add broth to skillet; increase heat to medium-high. Cook, stirring to loosen browned bits from pan; remove from heat.

3. Meanwhile, in another skillet, heat oil over medium-high heat. Add shallots, salt and pepper; cook and stir until shallots are tender. Add broth, stirring to loosen browned bits from pan. Stir in vinegar and jam. Bring to a boil; cook until slightly thickened, 4-5 minutes, stirring occasionally.

4. Slice the tenderloins; drizzle with pan juices. Serve with the berry sauce.

1 serving: 258 cal., 6g fat (0 sat. fat), 68mg chol., 414mg sod., 12g carb. (8g sugars, 0 fiber), 43g pro.
Diabetic exchanges: 5 lean meat, 1 starch, ½ fat.

SPICY APRICOT-GLAZED CHICKEN

Save yourself a trip to the store and check the fridge first. Chicken turns sweet and hot when you pull out the chili sauce, hot mustard and apricot preserves.

—Sonya Labbe,
West Hollywood, CA

Takes: 20 min.
Makes: 4 servings

- 1/3 cup apricot preserves
- 1/4 cup chili sauce
- 1 Tbsp. hot mustard
- 1/4 tsp. salt
- 1/8 tsp. pepper
- 4 boneless skinless chicken breast halves (4 oz. each)

1. Preheat broiler. In a small saucepan, combine the first 5 ingredients; cook and stir over medium heat until heated through.

2. Place chicken in a 15x10x1-in. baking pan coated with cooking spray. Broil 3-4 in. from heat until a thermometer reads 165°, 6-8 minutes on each side. Brush the chicken occasionally with preserves mixture during the last 5 minutes of cooking.

1 chicken breast half : 209 cal., 3g fat (1g sat. fat), 63mg chol., 476mg sod., 23g carb. (13g sugars, 0 fiber), 23g pro.

SPICY APRICOT-GLAZED CHICKEN

HONEY MUSTARD APPLE CHICKEN SAUSAGE

HONEY MUSTARD APPLE CHICKEN SAUSAGE

I threw this recipe together one day for a fantastic lunch. It's a good way to use up leftover sausage and rice from dinner the night before.
—Julie Puderbaugh, Berwick, PA

Takes: 20 min.
Makes: 4 servings

- ¼ cup honey mustard
- 2 Tbsp. apple jelly
- 1 Tbsp. water
- 1 Tbsp. olive oil
- 2 medium apples, sliced
- 1 pkg. (12 oz.) fully cooked apple chicken sausage links or flavor of your choice, sliced
- Hot cooked rice

1. In a small bowl, whisk honey mustard, jelly and water until blended. In a large skillet, heat oil over medium heat. Add the apples; cook and stir 2-3 minutes or until tender. Remove from the pan.
2. Add sausage to skillet; cook and stir 2-4 minutes or until browned. Return apples to skillet. Add mustard mixture; cook and stir 1-2 minutes or until thickened. Serve with rice.
¾ cup sausage mixture: 288 cal., 12g fat (3g sat. fat), 61mg chol., 609mg sod., 34g carb. (28g sugars, 2g fiber), 15g pro.

GLAZED SPATCHCOCKED CHICKEN

A few pantry items led to this change-of-pace entree. Try it any night of the week.
—James Schend, Pleasant Prairie, WI

Prep: 15 min.
Grill: 40 minutes + standing
Makes: 6 servings

- 1 cup white wine or chicken broth
- 1 cup apricot preserves or quince jelly
- 1 Tbsp. stone-ground mustard
- 1 broiler/fryer chicken (3 to 4 lbs.)
- ¾ tsp. salt
- ½ tsp. pepper

1. In a small saucepan, bring wine to a boil; cook 3-4 minutes or until wine is reduced by half. Stir in preserves and mustard. Reserve half of glaze for basting.
2. Cut the chicken along each side of the backbone with shears. Remove the backbone. Turn the chicken breast side up, and press to flatten. Sprinkle with salt and pepper.
3. Prepare grill for indirect medium heat. Place chicken on greased grill grate, skin side down, covered, over direct heat 10-15 minutes or until nicely browned. Turn the chicken and place over indirect heat until a thermometer reads 170°-175° in the thickest part of the thigh, brushing occasionally with reserved glaze mixture, about 30 minutes.
4. Remove chicken from grill. Let stand 15 minutes before carving; serve with remaining glaze.
5 oz. cooked chicken: 437 cal., 17g fat (5g sat. fat), 104mg chol., 458mg sod., 35g carb. (23g sugars, 0 fiber), 34g pro.

GLAZED SPATCHCOCKED CHICKEN

SWEET & SPICY CHIPOTLE CHICKEN

My husband and I have created many wonderful memories through sharing this meal with our friends. In the winter, we bake it indoors; in the summer, it works well on the grill, too! Either way the chicken pretty much cooks itself, leaving you plenty of time to visit with friends and family.

—Ashlie Delshad,
West Lafayette, IN

Prep: 15 min. + marinating
Bake: 1 hour 50 min. + standing
Makes: 8 servings

- 2 chipotle peppers in adobo sauce plus 3 Tbsp. adobo sauce
- ¼ cup tomato paste
- 3 Tbsp. honey
- 2 Tbsp. olive oil
- 1 tsp. sea salt
- 1 roasting chicken (6 to 7 lbs.)

1. Pulse the chipotle peppers, adobo sauce, tomato paste, honey, olive oil and sea salt in a food processor or blender until smooth. Spread mixture evenly over the chicken. Refrigerate, covered, at least 1 hour or overnight.

2. Preheat oven to 400°. Place chicken on a rack in a shallow roasting pan, breast side up. Tuck wings under chicken; tie drumsticks together.

3. Roast 20 minutes. Reduce oven setting to 350°. Roast 1½-1¾ hours longer or until a thermometer inserted in thickest part of thigh reads 170°-175°. (Cover loosely with foil if the chicken browns too quickly.)

4. Remove the chicken from oven; tent with foil. Let stand 15 minutes before carving. If desired, skim the fat and thicken pan drippings for gravy. Serve with chicken.

6 oz. cooked chicken: 462 cal., 27g fat (7g sat. fat), 134mg chol., 437mg sod., 9g carb. (8g sugars,

TEST KITCHEN TIP

Shred any leftover chicken with two forks and mix with extra gravy. Stuff into flour tortillas with fresh greens and bit of salsa and cheese for a quick and easy lunch.

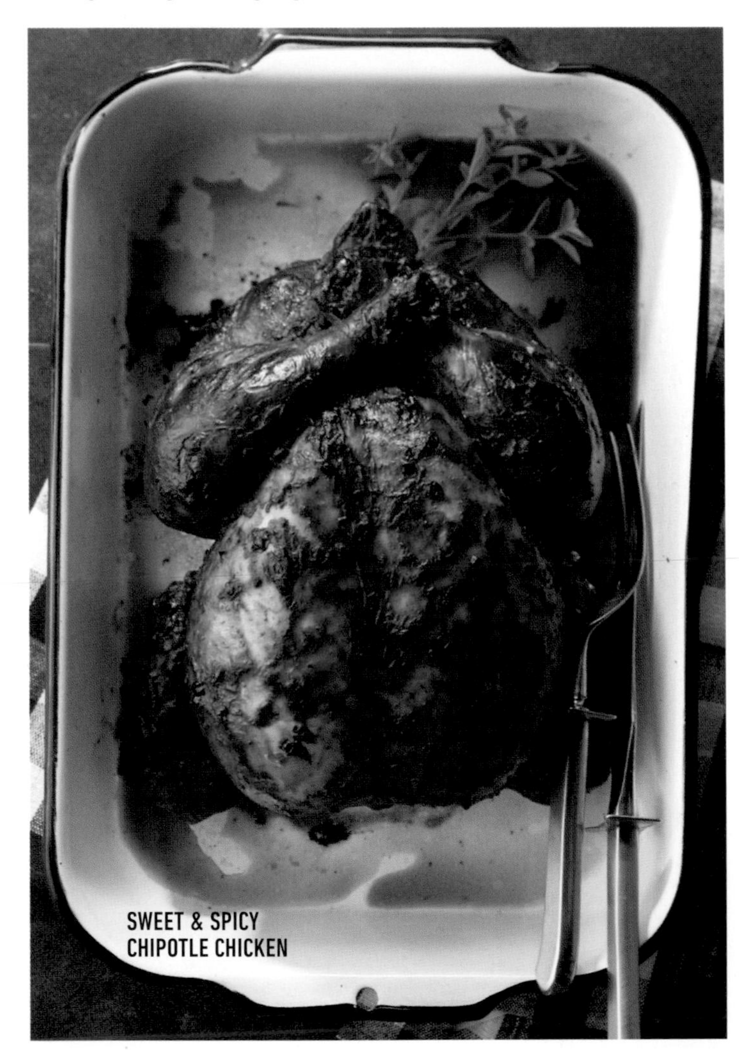

SWEET & SPICY CHIPOTLE CHICKEN

PRESSURE-COOKER PINEAPPLE CHICKEN

PRESSURE-COOKER PINEAPPLE CHICKEN

We love Hawaiian-style chicken that's made in a slow cooker, but sometimes we need a dinner that comes together fast. We tweaked our favorite recipe to work in a pressure cooker for a quick and easy weeknight meal. Add a side salad for a complete meal.
—Courtney Stultz, Weir, KS

Prep: 10 min.
Cook: 20 min. + releasing
Makes: 6 servings

- 1½ lbs. boneless skinless chicken breasts
- 1 can (20 oz.) unsweetened pineapple chunks, undrained
- ¼ cup barbecue sauce
- 1 cup chicken broth
- 1 cup uncooked long grain brown rice
- ½ tsp. salt
- Optional: Minced fresh cilantro and sliced green onions

1. Combine the first 6 ingredients in a 6-qt. electric pressure cooker. Lock lid; close pressure-release valve. Adjust to pressure-cook on high for 20 minutes.

2. Let pressure release naturally. Remove chicken to a cutting board and shred with 2 forks. Add shredded chicken back to the pot and stir until combined. If desired, sprinkle with cilantro and green onions.

1 cup: 313 cal., 4g fat (1g sat. fat), 63mg chol., 536mg sod., 41g carb. (16g sugars, 3g fiber), 27g pro. **Diabetic exchanges:** 3 lean meat, 2½ starch.

PANCETTA & MUSHROOM-STUFFED CHICKEN BREAST

I was inspired by a restaurant's Marsala and wanted to come up with my own.

—Ashley Laymon, Lititz, PA

Prep: 15 min. • **Bake:** 30 min.
Makes: 4 servings

- 4 slices pancetta
- 1 Tbsp. olive oil
- 1 shallot, finely chopped
- ¾ cup chopped fresh mushrooms
- ¼ tsp. salt, divided
- ¼ tsp. pepper, divided
- 4 boneless skinless chicken breast halves (6 oz. each)
- ½ cup prepared pesto

1. Preheat oven to 350°. In a large skillet, cook pancetta over medium heat until partially cooked but not crisp; drain on paper towels.

2. In same skillet, heat oil over medium-high heat. Add the shallot; cook and stir until lightly browned, 1-2 minutes. Stir in mushrooms; cook until tender, 1-2 minutes. Add ⅛ tsp. salt and ⅛ tsp. pepper.

3. Pound chicken breasts with a mallet to ¼-in. thickness. Spread each with 2 Tbsp. pesto; layer with 1 slice pancetta and a fourth of the mushroom mixture. Fold chicken in half, enclosing filling; secure with toothpicks. Sprinkle with remaining salt and pepper.

4. Transfer to a greased 13x9-in. baking dish. Bake chicken until a thermometer inserted in chicken reads 165°, 30-35 minutes. Discard all of the toothpicks before serving.

1 stuffed chicken breast half: 420 cal., 25g fat (6g sat. fat), 112mg chol., 1013mg sod., 5g carb. (2g sugars, 1g fiber), 41g pro.

TEST KITCHEN TIP
For those who don't like mushrooms, substitute 1 cup baby spinach and saute with shallots.

CHEESY ONION CHICKEN SKILLET

My zesty chicken with peppers and onions is so versatile, it works when you serve it over rice, potatoes, noodles, even a hoagie bun.
—Kim Johnson, Sibley, IA

Takes: 20 min.
Makes: 4 servings

- 1 lb. boneless skinless chicken breasts, cubed
- 2 tsp. Mrs. Dash Garlic & Herb seasoning blend
- 2 Tbsp. olive oil, divided
- 1 medium green pepper, cut into strips
- ½ medium onion, sliced
- 1 cup shredded Colby-Monterey Jack cheese

1. Toss chicken with seasoning blend. In a large nonstick skillet, heat 1 Tbsp. oil over medium-high heat. Add the chicken; cook and stir 5-7 minutes or until no longer pink. Remove from pan. In same pan, add the remaining oil, pepper and onion; cook and stir 3-4 minutes or until crisp-tender.
2. Stir in the chicken; sprinkle with cheese. Remove from heat; let stand, covered, until the cheese is melted.
1¼ cups: 293 cal., 17g fat (8g sat. fat), 88mg chol., 226mg sod., 4g carb. (1g sugars, 1g fiber), 29g pro.

CHEESY ONION CHICKEN SKILLET

ROMANO BASIL TURKEY BREAST

ROMANO BASIL TURKEY BREAST

Guests will be impressed when you slice this golden, grilled turkey breast, dressed up with a flavorful layer of basil and cheese under the skin.
—Darlene Markham, Rochester, NY

Prep: 15 min.
Grill: 1½ hours + standing
Makes: 8 servings

- 1 cup Romano cheese, shredded
- ½ cup fresh basil leaves, chopped
- 4 lemon slices
- 4 garlic cloves, minced
- 1 bone-in turkey breast (4 to 5 lbs.)
- 2 Tbsp. olive oil
- ½ tsp. salt
- ¼ tsp. pepper

1. Combine the cheese, basil, lemon slices and garlic. With fingers, carefully loosen skin from the turkey breast; place mixture under the skin. Secure skin to underside of breast with toothpicks. Rub skin with oil and sprinkle with salt and pepper.
2. Prepare grill for indirect heat, using a drip pan. Place turkey over drip pan. Grill, covered, over indirect medium heat until a thermometer reads 170°, 1½-2 hours. Remove toothpicks. Cover and let the turkey stand for 10 minutes before slicing.
6 oz. cooked turkey: 402 cal., 20g fat (7g sat. fat), 136mg chol., 493mg sod., 1g carb. (0 sugars, 0 fiber), 53g pro.

BROILED CHICKEN & ARTICHOKES

BROILED CHICKEN & ARTICHOKES

My wife and I first made this chicken entree as newlyweds, and we have been hooked on it ever since. We make it almost weekly now. It's so simple and affordable yet delicious and healthy. Can't beat that!
—Chris Koon, Midlothian, VA

Takes: 15 min.
Makes: 8 servings

- 8 boneless skinless chicken thighs (about 2 lbs.)
- 2 jars (7½ oz. each) marinated quartered artichoke hearts, drained
- 2 Tbsp. olive oil
- 1 tsp. salt
- ½ tsp. pepper
- ¼ cup shredded Parmesan cheese
- 2 Tbsp. minced fresh parsley

1. Preheat broiler. In a large bowl, toss the chicken and artichokes with oil, salt and pepper. Transfer to a broiler pan.
2. Broil 3 in. from the heat for 8-10 minutes or until a thermometer inserted in the chicken reads 170°, turning chicken and artichokes halfway through cooking. Sprinkle with cheese. Broil 1-2 minutes longer or until cheese is melted. Sprinkle with parsley.
1 serving: 288 cal., 21g fat (5g sat. fat), 77mg chol., 584mg sod., 4g carb. (0 sugars, 0 fiber), 22g pro.

PRESSURE-COOKER SPICY LIME CHICKEN

This tender chicken with light lime flavor is a natural filling for tacos, but my son Austin also loves it spooned over cooked rice and sprinkled with his favorite taco toppings.
—Christine Hair, Odessa, FL

Prep: 10 min. • **Cook:** 10 min.
Makes: 6 servings

- 4 boneless skinless chicken breast halves (6 oz. each)
- 2 cups chicken broth
- 3 Tbsp. lime juice
- 1 Tbsp. chili powder
- 1 tsp. grated lime zest
- Fresh cilantro leaves, optional

1. Place chicken in a 6-qt. electric pressure cooker. Combine broth, lime juice and chili powder; pour over chicken. Lock lid; close pressure-release valve. Adjust to pressure-cook on high for 6 minutes.

2. Quick-release pressure. A thermometer inserted in chicken should read at least 165°.

3. Remove chicken. When cool enough to handle, shred meat with 2 forks; return to pressure cooker. Stir in lime zest. If desired, serve with cilantro.

Freeze option: Freeze cooled meat mixture in freezer containers. To use, partially thaw in refrigerator overnight. Microwave, covered, on high in a microwave-safe dish until heated through, stirring occasionally; add broth if necessary.

1 serving: 132 cal., 3g fat (1g sat. fat), 64mg chol., 420mg sod., 2g carb. (1g sugars, 1g fiber), 23g pro. **Diabetic exchanges:** 3 lean meat.

★★★★★ **READER REVIEW**

"Great base recipe! Simple and easy recipe that would be perfect for tacos, salads, enchiladas or, as suggested, burrito bowls. That's what we did, and my family loved them!"
—JSTOWELLSUPERMOM, TASTEOFHOME.COM

SLOW-COOKER LUAU CHICKEN

As long as you're cooking bacon for breakfast, save some for the slow cooker. In four short hours, you'll be saying "aloha" to lunch.
—Cindy Lund, Valley Center, CA

Prep: 15 min. • **Cook:** 4 hours
Makes: 6 servings

- 6 bacon strips, divided
- 6 boneless skinless chicken thighs (about 1½ lbs.)
- ¼ tsp. salt
- ⅛ tsp. pepper
- ½ cup chopped red onion
- 1 cup crushed pineapple, drained
- ¾ cup barbecue sauce

1. Cut 3 bacon strips in half; cook until partially cooked but not crisp. Drain on paper towels.
2. Season the chicken with the salt and pepper; place in a 3-qt. slow cooker. Top each thigh with a half piece of bacon. Top with the onion, pineapple and barbecue sauce.
3. Cover and cook on low for 4-5 hours or until chicken is tender. Cook remaining bacon until crisp; drain and crumble. Sprinkle over each serving.

1 serving: 375 cal., 17g fat (5g sat. fat), 135mg chol., 637mg sod., 14g carb. (13g sugars, 1g fiber), 39g pro.

Slow-Cooker Ginger-Peach Chicken: Omit bacon, salt, pepper, onion, pineapple and barbecue sauce. Place chicken in slow cooker. Top with ¾ cup sliced peeled fresh or thawed frozen peaches and ¾ cup golden raisins. Mix ¾ cup peach preserves, ¼ cup chili sauce, 4 tsp. minced crystallized ginger, 2 tsp. minced garlic cloves and 2 tsp. reduced- sod. soy sauce. Spoon over top. Cook as the recipe directs.

AFRICAN CHICKEN & SWEET POTATOES

I came up with this when I combined some of my favorite ingredients: sweet potatoes, chicken and peanut butter. Add mango chutney and tomatoes, and you've got a fantastic busy-week recipe.

—Devon Delaney, Westport, CT

Prep: 10 min. • **Bake:** 40 min.
Makes: 6 servings

- 6 bone-in chicken thighs (about 2¼ lbs.)
- ½ tsp. salt
- ¼ tsp. pepper
- 2 Tbsp. canola oil
- 2 medium sweet potatoes, peeled and finely chopped (about 4 cups)
- ½ cup mango chutney
- ¼ cup creamy peanut butter
- 1 can (10 oz.) diced tomatoes and green chiles, undrained

1. Preheat oven to 375°. Place chicken in a greased 13x9-in. baking dish; sprinkle with salt and pepper. Bake, uncovered, 30 minutes.

2. Meanwhile, in a large skillet, heat oil over medium-high heat. Add sweet potatoes; cook and stir 10-12 minutes or until tender. In a small bowl, mix chutney and peanut butter; stir into the sweet potatoes. Add tomatoes; heat through.

3. Spoon potato mixture over chicken. Bake 10-15 minutes longer or until a thermometer inserted in chicken reads 170°-175°.

1 chicken thigh with ½ cup potato mixture: 480 cal., 24g fat (5g sat. fat), 81 mg chol., 733mg sod., 38g carb. (19g sugars, 3g fiber), 26g pro.

GLAZED CORNISH HENS

If you're looking to add a touch of elegance to your dinner table, our Test Kitchen *home economists suggest these Cornish game hens topped with a sweet apricot glaze.*
—*Taste of Home* Test Kitchen

Prep: 5 min. • **Bake:** 1 hour
Makes: 4 servings

- 2 Cornish game hens (20 to 24 oz. each), split lengthwise
- ¼ tsp. salt
- ⅛ tsp. white pepper
- ⅓ cup apricot spreadable fruit
- 1 Tbsp. orange juice

1. Preheat oven to 350°. Place hens, breast side up, on a rack in a shallow roasting pan. Sprinkle with salt and pepper. Bake hens, uncovered, 30 minutes.
2. In a small bowl, combine spreadable fruit and orange juice. Spoon some of apricot mixture over the hens. Bake until golden brown and juices run clear, 30-35 minutes, basting several times with remaining apricot mixture. Let stand 5 minutes before serving.
½ hen: 402 cal., 24g fat (7g sat. fat), 175mg chol., 233mg sod., 14g carb. (11g sugars, 0 fiber), 30g pro.

GLAZED CORNISH HENS

DINNER POPPERS

DINNER POPPERS

I could eat jalapeno poppers all day long, but who wants to say they had seven stuffed peppers for dinner? For this delicious meal-in-one, I use poblanos for my husband and son, and hotter peppers for me and my daughter.
—Sherri Jerzyk, Somerville, TX

Prep: 20 min. • **Bake:** 25 min.
Makes: 4 servings

- 4 bacon strips
- 4 chicken tenderloins
- ¼ tsp. salt
- ⅛ tsp. pepper
- 2 tsp. canola oil
- 4 poblano peppers
- 1½ cups shredded cheddar cheese, divided
- 4 oz. cream cheese, cut into 4 strips

1. Preheat oven to 350°. In a large skillet, cook bacon over medium heat until partially cooked but not crisp. Remove to paper towels to drain.
2. Sprinkle chicken with salt and pepper. In a skillet, heat oil over medium-high heat; brown tenderloins on both sides. Cool slightly.
3. Carefully cut a slit down the side of each pepper and remove seeds. Fill each with 1 chicken tenderloin; top each with 2 Tbsp. cheese and a strip of cream cheese. Close the peppers; wrap with bacon and secure with toothpicks.
4. Place on a foil-lined baking sheet, slit side up. Top with remaining cheddar cheese; bake until browned and peppers are tender, 25-30 minutes. Remove toothpicks before serving.
1 serving: 389 cal., 30g fat (15g sat. fat), 96mg chol., 682mg sod., 9g carb. (4g sugars, 2g fiber), 23g pro.

TURKEY SCALLOPINI WITH MARSALA SAUCE

My family requests this entree at least once a month. The slightly sweet Marsala sauce is delicious over the turkey slices.
—Briana Knight, Ferndale, WA

Takes: 30 min.
Makes: 4 servings

- ½ cup all-purpose flour
- ½ tsp. salt
- ½ tsp. pepper
- 1 pkg. (17.6 oz.) turkey breast cutlets
- 2 Tbsp. olive oil
- 1½ cups Marsala wine
- 3 Tbsp. butter
- 3 Tbsp. shredded Parmesan cheese
- Hot cooked linguine, optional

1. In a large resealable bag or another container, mix flour, salt and pepper. Add turkey cutlets, one at a time, close bag and shake to coat.
2. In a large skillet; heat oil over medium heat. Add turkey; cook 3-4 minutes on each side or until meat is no longer pink. Remove from pan. Stir in wine. Bring to a boil; cook 8-10 minutes or until liquid is reduced to about ½ cup. Stir in butter until melted. Return turkey to pan; heat through. Serve with cheese and, if desired, linguine.
1 serving: 459 cal., 17g fat (7g sat. fat), 103mg chol., 341mg sod., 18g carb. (7g sugars, 0 fiber), 33g pro.

TURKEY SCALLOPINI
WITH MARSALA SAUCE

BAKED BUFFALO CHICKEN

When I make this tangy chicken, I have to double the recipe because it disappears so fast. Better to have leftovers, especially as they make ideal sandwiches and salads.

—Beth Zimmerman, Willingboro, NJ

Prep: 20 min. + marinating
Bake: 25 min. • **Makes:** 4 servings

- ¾ cup Buffalo wing sauce, divided
- 4 boneless skinless chicken breast halves (6 oz. each)
- ¾ cup all-purpose flour
- ¾ tsp. dried tarragon
- ½ tsp. pepper
- 1¼ cups panko bread crumbs

1. Pour ⅓ cup o the wing sauce into a shallow dish. Add the chicken breasts and turn to coat. Let chicken stand for 15 minutes or refrigerate, covered, up to 24 hours.

2. Preheat oven to 400°. Drain chicken, discarding marinade. In a shallow bowl, mix flour, tarragon and pepper. Place bread crumbs and remaining wing sauce in separate shallow bowls. Dip chicken in flour mixture to coat all sides; shake off excess. Dip in wing sauce, then in bread crumbs, patting to help coating adhere.

3. Place chicken on a rack in a 15x10x1-in. baking pan. Bake 25-30 minutes or until a thermometer reads 165°.

1 chicken breast half : 277 cal., 5g fat (1g sat. fat), 94mg chol., 811mg sod., 18g carb. (1g sugars, 1g fiber), 37g pro. **Diabetic exchanges:** 5 lean meat, 1 starch.

BAKED BUFFALO CHICKEN

TEST KITCHEN TIP

It's worth it to keep plenty of dinner ingredients on hand. Buy chicken breasts in bulk and freeze them so you always have a protein handy when time is tight.

STUFFED CHICKEN WITH MARINATED TOMATOES

STUFFED CHICKEN WITH MARINATED TOMATOES

I invented this entree to prove how delicious goat cheese really is. I served it to my skeptical family, and they gobbled it up.

—Gilda Lester, Millsboro, DE

Prep: 15 min. + marinating
Bake: 20 min. • **Makes:** 4 servings

- 4 boneless skinless chicken breast halves (6 oz. each)
- ¾ cup Italian salad dressing, divided
- 1 log (4 oz.) fresh goat cheese
- ¼ tsp. salt
- ⅛ tsp. pepper
- 2 cups grape tomatoes, quartered
- ½ cup thinly sliced fresh basil

1. Cut a pocket horizontally in the thickest part of each chicken breast; place in a bowl. Toss with ¼ cup dressing; refrigerate, covered, 30 minutes.

2. Preheat oven to 425°. Crumble goat cheese; reserve ½ cup goat cheese for serving. Divide the remaining cheese among the chicken pockets; secure with toothpicks. Place in a greased 15x10x1-in. pan; sprinkle with salt and pepper.

3. Roast until a thermometer inserted in the chicken reads 165°, 20-25 minutes. Toss tomatoes with remaining dressing; let stand while chicken is cooking.

4. Add basil to tomato mixture; serve over chicken. Top with remaining cheese.

1 serving: 334 cal., 14g fat (4g sat. fat), 113mg chol., 797mg sod., 7g carb. (5g sugars, 1g fiber), 38g pro.

BACON & CHEDDAR CHICKEN

BACON & CHEDDAR CHICKEN

Cheese and bacon don't usually come light but this tasty recipe keeps the fat and calories low. Best of all, the 30-minute family-friendly recipe can be doubled to serve larger groups.
—Trisha Kruse, Eagle, ID

Takes: 30 min.
Makes: 4 servings

- 4 bacon strips, chopped
- 4 boneless skinless chicken breast halves (6 oz. each)
- ¼ tsp. salt
- ¼ tsp. pepper
- ⅔ cup barbecue sauce, divided
- ½ cup shredded cheddar cheese
- Thinly sliced green onions

1. Preheat oven to 350°. In a cast-iron or other ovenproof skillet, cook the bacon over medium heat until crisp, stirring occasionally. Using a slotted spoon, remove bacon to paper towels; reserve drippings.
2. Sprinkle chicken with salt and pepper. In the same pan, brown chicken in drippings over medium heat, 3-4 minutes per side. Brush with ⅓ cup barbecue sauce. Transfer to oven; bake 8 minutes.
3. Spoon remaining sauce over chicken; sprinkle with cheese and bacon. Bake until cheese is melted and a thermometer reads 165°, 4-6 minutes. Sprinkle with green onions.

1 chicken breast half: 435 cal., 20g fat (8g sat. fat), 126mg chol., 973mg sod., 19g carb. (15g sugars, 0 fiber), 41g pro.

TURKEY CUTLETS IN LEMON WINE SAUCE

After I tried something similar while dining out, I learned how to make it at home. Now I serve it a lot since it's so quick to make—and my family is so happy I do.

—Kathie Wilson, Warrenton, VA

Takes: 25 min.
Makes: 4 servings

- ½ cup all-purpose flour
- ½ tsp. salt
- ½ tsp. paprika
- ¼ tsp. pepper
- 4 turkey breast cutlets (2½ oz. each)
- 1 Tbsp. olive oil
- 1 cup white wine or chicken broth
- ¼ cup lemon juice

1. In a shallow bowl, mix flour, salt, paprika and pepper. Dip turkey in flour mixture to coat both sides; shake off excess.
2. In a large skillet, heat oil over medium heat. Add turkey and cook in batches 1-2 minutes on each side or until no longer pink. Remove from pan.
3. Add wine and lemon juice to skillet, stirring to loosen browned bits. Bring to a boil; cook until liquid is reduced by half. Return cutlets to pan; turn to coat and heat through.

1 turkey cutlet with 2 Tbsp. sauce: 145 cal., 4g fat (1g sat. fat), 44mg chol., 110mg sod., 5g carb. (1g sugars, 0 fiber), 18g pro. **Diabetic exchanges:** 2 lean meat, 1 fat.

TURKEY CUTLETS IN LEMON WINE SAUCE

WHITE WINE GARLIC CHICKEN

WHITE WINE GARLIC CHICKEN

This garlic chicken is fantastic over cooked brown rice or your favorite pasta. Don't forget a sprinkle of Parmesan or Asiago cheese, too.

—Heather Esposito, Rome, NY

Takes: 30 min.
Makes: 4 servings

- 4 boneless skinless chicken breast halves (6 oz. each)
- ½ tsp. salt
- ¼ tsp. pepper
- 1 Tbsp. olive oil
- 2 cups sliced baby portobello mushrooms (about 6 oz.)
- 1 medium onion, chopped
- 2 garlic cloves, minced
- ½ cup dry white wine or reduced-sodium chicken broth

1. Pound chicken breasts with a meat mallet to ½-in. thickness; sprinkle with salt and pepper. In a large skillet, heat oil over medium heat; cook chicken until no longer pink, 5-6 minutes per side. Remove from pan; keep warm.

2. Add mushrooms and onion to pan; cook and stir over medium-high heat until tender and lightly browned, 2-3 minutes. Add the garlic; cook and stir 30 seconds. Add wine; bring to a boil, stirring to loosen browned bits from the pan. Cook until liquid is slightly reduced, 1-2 minutes; serve over the chicken.

1 chicken breast half with ¼ cup mushroom mixture: 243 cal., 7g fat (2g sat. fat), 94mg chol., 381mg sod., 5g carb. (2g sugars, 1g fiber), 36g pro. **Diabetic exchanges:** 5 lean meat, 1 fat.

AIR-FRYER CRISPY CURRY DRUMSTICKS

AIR-FRYER CRISPY CURRY DRUMSTICKS

These air-fryer chicken drumsticks are flavorful, crispy on the outside and juicy on the inside. Sometimes I'll add a dash of red pepper flakes in addition to the curry powder if I want to spice them up a little bit. I like to serve them with chicken-seasoned rice and boiled broccoli.

—Zena Furgason, Norman, OK

Prep: 35 min.
Cook: 15 min./batch
Makes: 4 servings

- 1 lb. chicken drumsticks
- ¾ tsp. salt, divided
- 2 Tbsp. olive oil
- 2 tsp. curry powder
- ½ tsp. onion salt
- ½ tsp. garlic powder
- Minced fresh cilantro, optional

1. Place chicken in a large bowl; add ½ tsp. salt and enough water to cover. Let stand 15 minutes at room temperature. Drain and pat dry.

2. Preheat air fryer to 375°. In another bowl, mix oil, curry powder, onion salt, garlic powder and remaining ¼ tsp. salt; add chicken and toss to coat. In batches, place chicken in a single layer on tray in greased air-fryer basket. Cook until a thermometer inserted in chicken reads 170°-175°, 15-17 minutes, turning halfway. If desired, sprinkle with cilantro.

2 oz. cooked chicken: 180 cal., 13g fat (3g sat. fat), 47mg chol., 711mg sod., 1g carb. (0 sugars, 1g fiber), 15g pro.

BBQ & RANCH CHICKEN PIZZA

I wanted something different for dinner and came up with this pizza. Everyone loved it! Best of all, it takes advantage of leftover chicken and convenience items.

—Sue Sitler, Bloomsburg, PA

Takes: 30 min.
Makes: 8 servings

- 2 tubes (8 oz. each) refrigerated crescent rolls
- ½ cup hickory smoke-flavored barbecue sauce, divided
- ¼ cup prepared ranch salad dressing
- 3 cups cubed cooked chicken breasts
- 2 cups shredded pizza cheese blend

1. Preheat oven to 375°. Unroll both tubes of crescent dough and press onto the bottom and up the sides of an ungreased 15x10x1-in. baking pan, pressing perforations to seal. Bake 8-10 minutes or until lightly browned.

2. In a small bowl, mix ¼ cup barbecue sauce and salad dressing; spread over crust. In another bowl, toss chicken with remaining barbecue sauce. Arrange over top. Sprinkle with cheese. Bake 15-20 minutes longer or until crust is golden brown and cheese is melted.

1 piece: 431 cal., 22g fat (5g sat. fat), 66mg chol., 875mg sod., 32g carb. (12g sugars, 0 fiber), 25g pro.

CRISPY BUFFALO CHICKEN ROLL-UPS

These winning chicken rolls with a crispy crust are both impressive and easy to make. They're so tasty! My family and friends absolutely love them!

—Lisa Keys, Kennet Square, PA

Prep: 15 min. • **Bake:** 30 min.
Makes: 4 servings

- 4 boneless skinless chicken breast halves (6 oz. each)
- ¾ tsp. salt
- ½ tsp. pepper
- ¼ cup crumbled blue cheese
- ¼ cup hot pepper sauce
- 2 Tbsp. mayonnaise
- 1 cup crushed cornflakes

1. Preheat oven to 400°. Flatten the chicken breasts to ¼-in. thickness. Season with the salt and pepper; sprinkle with the blue cheese. Roll up each from a short side and secure with toothpicks.

2. In a shallow bowl, combine pepper sauce and mayonnaise. Place cornflakes in a separate shallow bowl. Dip the chicken in pepper sauce mixture, then coat with cornflakes. Place seam side down in a greased 11x7-in. baking dish.

3. Bake, uncovered, 30-35 minutes or until chicken is no longer pink. Discard toothpicks.

1 serving: 270 cal., 8g fat (3g sat. fat), 101mg chol., 764mg sod., 10g carb. (1g sugars, 0 fiber), 37g pro.

CRISPY BUFFALO CHICKEN ROLL-UPS

SUN-DRIED TOMATO TURKEY BURGERS

This recipe always brings back fond memories of homemade sun-dried tomatoes my mom made each summer. I have prepared this with ground beef and ground turkey. Either way, it's fast and tastes delicious!
—Sammy Staab, Pensacola, FL

Takes: 25 min.
Makes: 6 servings

- 1 large red onion
- 1 cup (4 oz.) crumbled feta cheese, divided
- ⅔ cup chopped oil-packed sun-dried tomatoes
- ¼ tsp. salt
- ¼ tsp. pepper
- 2 lbs. lean ground turkey
- 6 ciabatta rolls, split

1. Cut onion in half. Finely chop one half and thinly slice the remaining half. Combine ½ cup feta, the sun-dried tomatoes, chopped onion, salt and pepper in a large bowl. Crumble turkey over mixture and mix lightly but thoroughly. Shape into 6 patties.
2. Grill burgers, covered, over medium heat or broil 4 in. from the heat for 5-7 minutes on each side or until a thermometer reads 165° and juices run clear.
3. Meanwhile, in a small nonstick skillet coated with cooking spray, saute sliced onion until tender. Serve burgers on buns with onion and remaining feta.

1 burger: 1073 cal., 46g fat (14g sat. fat), 169mg chol., 1518mg sod., 116g carb. (8g sugars, 8g fiber), 57g pro.

PORK, HAM & MORE

ROSEMARY-THYME LAMB CHOPS
P. 130

MIX UP YOUR MEALTIME ROUTINE WITH ANY OF THESE SAVORY, FAST-TO-FIX ENTREES.

CRANBERRY GLAZED
PORK CHOPS

CRANBERRY GLAZED PORK CHOPS

This main dish is simple enough for a weeknight, but the cranberries also make it a perfect choice for Christmas. It's colorful, juicy and easy. It comes together in less than half an hour so you're out of the kitchen and with your family at the table in no time.

—Roxanne Chan, Albany, CA

Takes: 25 min.
Makes: 4 servings

- 4 boneless pork loin chops (5 oz. each)
- ¼ tsp. salt
- ¼ tsp. pepper
- 1 cup fresh or frozen cranberries, thawed
- ⅓ cup water
- ⅓ cup sweet chili sauce
- 1 green onion, finely chopped

1. Sprinkle pork chops with salt and pepper. Heat a large skillet over medium heat. Add the pork; cook 4-6 minutes on each side or until a thermometer reads 145°. Remove from pan; keep warm.
2. In the same skillet, add the cranberries, water and chili sauce. Bring to a boil; cook, uncovered, 4-6 minutes or until the berries pop, stirring occasionally. Serve with pork chops; sprinkle with onion.

1 pork chop with 2 Tbsp. sauce: 248 cal., 8g fat (3g sat. fat), 68mg chol., 528mg sod., 14g carb. (12g sugars, 1g fiber), 28g pro.

SOUTHWESTERN PINEAPPLE PORK CHOPS

SOUTHWESTERN PINEAPPLE PORK CHOPS

This quick entree will instantly transport you to the Southwest. Salsa plays lively counterpoint to the pineapple-sweetened pork chops.

—Lisa Varner, El Paso, TX

Takes: 30 min.
Makes: 4 servings

- 4 boneless pork loin chops (5 oz. each)
- ½ tsp. garlic pepper blend
- 1 Tbsp. canola oil
- 1 can (8 oz.) unsweetened crushed pineapple, undrained
- 1 cup medium salsa
- Minced fresh cilantro

1. Sprinkle pork chops with pepper blend. In a large skillet, brown chops in oil. Remove and keep warm.
2. In the same skillet, combine crushed pineapple and salsa. Bring to a boil. Return pork chops to the pan. Reduce heat; cover and simmer 10-15 minutes or until a thermometer inserted into the pork reads 145°. Let pork stand 5 minutes before serving. Sprinkle with cilantro.

1 pork chop with ⅓ cup sauce: 274 cal., 12g fat (3g sat. fat), 68mg chol., 315mg sod., 13g carb. (9g sugars, 0 fiber), 27g pro. **Diabetic exchanges:** 4 lean meat, 1 fat, ½ fruit.

SWEET & SPICY JERK RIBS

Here's a no-fuss ribs recipe the whole family will love. The spicy rub and sweet sauce make it an instant favorite.

—Geri Lesch, New Port Richey, FL

Prep: 10 min. • **Cook:** 6 hours
Makes: 5 servings

- 4½ lbs. pork baby back ribs
- 3 Tbsp. olive oil
- ⅓ cup Caribbean jerk seasoning
- 3 cups honey barbecue sauce
- 3 Tbsp. apricot preserves
- 2 Tbsp. honey

1. Cut ribs into serving-sized pieces; brush with oil and rub with jerk seasoning. Place in a 5- or 6-qt. slow cooker. Combine the remaining ingredients; pour over ribs.
2. Cover and cook on low for 6-8 hours or until the meat is tender. Skim fat from sauce before serving.
1 serving: 1082 cal., 61g fat (21g sat. fat), 220mg chol., 2498mg sod., 77g carb. (64g sugars, 0 fiber), 45g pro.

PARMESAN-BREADED PORK CHOPS

The shredded Parmesan and seasoned bread crumbs push the flavor of these juicy chops over the top. The whole family loves this dish that cooks in the oven while I prepare the rest of the meal.

—Hayden Hosick, Corona, CA

Takes: 25 min.
Makes: 4 servings

- 4 boneless pork loin chops (6 oz. each)
- ½ tsp. salt
- ¼ tsp. pepper
- ½ cup garlic and herb bread crumbs
- ⅓ cup shredded Parmesan cheese
- 2 large eggs, lightly beaten
- 2 Tbsp. olive oil

1. Preheat oven to 350°. Sprinkle pork chops with salt and pepper. In a shallow bowl, mix bread crumbs and cheese. Place eggs in a separate shallow bowl. Dip pork chops in eggs, then in crumb mixture, patting to help coating adhere.
2. In a 10-in. ovenproof skillet, heat oil over medium heat. Brown pork chops on both sides. Bake 12-15 minutes or until a thermometer reads 145°. Let stand 5 minutes.
1 pork chop: 356 cal., 19g fat (6g sat. fat), 131mg chol., 577mg sod., 7g carb. (1g sugars, 0 fiber), 37g pro.

PARMESAN-BREADED PORK CHOPS

DIXIE LAMB CHOPS

These saucy lamb chops may seem fancy, but mine work for both special occasions and busy evenings. We love them with spinach salad and crusty bread.

—Barbara Burge, Los Gatos, CA

Takes: 20 min.
Makes: 4 servings

- 4 lamb loin chops (5 to 6 oz. each)
- ½ tsp. salt
- ¼ tsp. pepper
- 1 Tbsp. olive oil
- ¼ cup molasses
- 2 Tbsp. steak sauce
- 1 Tbsp. cider vinegar

1. Sprinkle lamb chops with salt and pepper. In a large skillet, heat oil over medium heat; cook chops, covered, until bottoms are browned, 5-7 minutes.
2. Mix molasses, steak sauce and vinegar. Turn chops; pour molasses mixture over top. Cook, covered, over medium-low heat until lamb reaches desired doneness (for medium-rare, a thermometer should read 135°; medium, 140°; medium-well, 145°), 5-7 minutes. Let stand 5 minutes before serving.

1 lamb chop with 1 Tbsp. glaze: 225 cal., 9g fat (3g sat. fat), 57mg chol., 493mg sod., 17g carb. (16g sugars, 0 fiber), 18g pro. **Diabetic exchanges:** 3 lean meat, 1 starch, ½ fat.

ITALIAN SMOTHERED PORK CHOPS

My brother and I come from an Italian family, and we designed these pork chops to include Italian staples such as fresh mozzarella, sweet red peppers and broccoli rabe.

—Shana Lewis, Totowa, NJ

Takes: 30 min.
Makes: 4 servings

- ½ lb. broccoli rabe
- 4 boneless pork loin chops (¾ in. thick and 6 oz. each)
- 1 tsp. salt
- 1 tsp. garlic powder
- ½ tsp. pepper
- 1 Tbsp. canola oil
- ½ cup sliced roasted sweet red pepper
- 4 oz. fresh mozzarella cheese, sliced

1. Preheat broiler. Trim ½ in. off ends of broccoli rabe; discard any coarse leaves.

2. In a large saucepan, bring 4 cups water to a boil. Add the broccoli rabe; cook, uncovered, 4-5 minutes or just until crisp-tender. Remove and immediately drop into ice water. Drain and pat dry.

3. Sprinkle pork chops with seasonings. In a broiler-safe skillet, heat oil over medium-high heat. Add the pork chops; cook 3-4 minutes on each side or until a thermometer reads 145°. Remove from heat.

4. Layer chops with red pepper, broccoli rabe and cheese. Broil 4 in. from heat 1-2 minutes or until cheese is melted.

1 serving: 365 cal., 20g fat (8g sat. fat), 104mg chol., 808mg sod., 4g carb. (2g sugars, 2g fiber), 40g pro.

JUST PEACHY PORK TENDERLOIN

I had a pork tenderloin and ripe peaches and decided to put them together. The results proved irresistible! Here's a fresh entree that tastes just like summer.

—Julia Gosliga, Addison, VT

Takes: 20 min.
Makes: 4 servings

- 1 lb. pork tenderloin, cut into 12 slices
- ½ tsp. salt
- ¼ tsp. pepper
- 2 tsp. olive oil
- 4 medium peaches, peeled and sliced
- 1 Tbsp. lemon juice
- ¼ cup peach preserves

1. Flatten each tenderloin slice to ¼-in. thickness. Sprinkle with salt and pepper. In a large nonstick skillet over medium heat, cook pork in oil until tender. Remove and keep warm.

2. Add peaches and lemon juice, stirring to loosen browned bits from pan. Cook and stir until peaches are tender, 3-4 minutes. Stir in the pork and preserves; heat through.

1 serving: 241 cal., 6g fat (2g sat. fat), 63mg chol., 340mg sod., 23g carb. (20g sugars, 2g fiber), 23g pro. **Diabetic exchanges:** 3 lean meat, 1 fruit, ½ starch, ½ fat.

JUST PEACHY PORK TENDERLOIN

PORK MEDALLIONS WITH RASPBERRY-BALSAMIC SAUCE

PORK MEDALLIONS WITH RASPBERRY-BALSAMIC SAUCE

Whenever I entertain, I prefer spending time with company to being stuck in the kitchen. This fast entree lets me serve a spectacular dinner with almost no hassle.

—Lisa Varner, El Paso, TX

Takes: 30 min.
Makes: 4 servings

- 1 pork tenderloin (1 lb.), cut into 1-in. slices
- 1 tsp. garlic powder
- 1 Tbsp. olive oil
- ½ cup seedless raspberry jam
- 2 Tbsp. balsamic vinegar
- 2 tsp. Dijon mustard

1. Flatten the pork to ½-in. thickness; sprinkle with the garlic powder.
2. In a large skillet over medium heat, cook the pork in oil until no longer pink, 3-5 minutes on each side. Remove and keep warm. Add the raspberry jam, vinegar and mustard to the pan. Cook and stir for 2-3 minutes or until thickened. Serve with pork.

3 oz. cooked pork with about 2 Tbsp. sauce: 271 cal., 7g fat (2g sat. fat), 63mg chol., 107mg sod., 28g carb. (25g sugars, 0 fiber), 23g pro.

HABANERO RASPBERRY RIBS

Roasting these tender ribs in the oven means you can enjoy them any time of year—no waiting for grilling season. The heat from the habanero pepper and the sweetness of the jam complement each other.

—Yvonne Roat, Linden, MI

Prep: 10 min.
Bake: 3 hours 10 min.
Makes: 5 servings

- 2 racks pork baby back ribs (about 4½ lbs.)
- 2½ cups barbecue sauce, divided
- 2 cups seedless raspberry jam
- 1 habanero pepper, finely chopped

1. Place each rack of ribs on a double thickness of heavy-duty foil (about 28x18 in.). Combine 2 cups of the barbecue sauce, raspberry jam and habanero; pour over ribs. Wrap the foil tightly around ribs.
2. Place in a shallow roasting pan. Bake at 325° for 3 hours or until meat is tender.
3. Carefully unwrap ribs. Place on baking sheets. Brush with remaining barbecue sauce. Broil 4 in. from the heat for 8-10 minutes or until bubbly. If desired, serve with additional barbecue sauce.

1 serving: 1067 cal., 38g fat (14g sat. fat), 147mg chol., 1562mg sod., 139g carb. (122g sugars, 1g fiber), 41g pro.

HABANERO RASPBERRY RIBS

GRILLED PORK CHOPS WITH STICKY SWEET SAUCE

GRILLED PORK CHOPS WITH STICKY SWEET SAUCE

How can you go wrong with these savory chops that call for only a handful of ingredients? Best of all, they're impressive enough to serve to guests!
—Angela Spengler, Niceville, FL

Takes: 30 min.
Makes: 4 servings

- ¼ cup molasses
- 1 Tbsp. Worcestershire sauce
- 1½ tsp. brown sugar
- 4 boneless pork loin chops (¾ in. thick and 5 oz. each)

1. In a small bowl, combine the molasses, Worcestershire sauce and brown sugar. Reserve 3 Tbsp. sauce for serving.
2. Grill the pork, covered, over medium heat or broil 4 in. from heat 4-5 minutes on each side or until a thermometer reads 145°, brushing with remaining sauce during the last 3 minutes of cooking. Let stand 5 minutes before serving. Serve with the reserved sauce.

1 pork chop with about 2 tsp. sauce: 256 cal., 8g fat (3g sat. fat), 68mg chol., 89mg sod., 17g carb. (13g sugars, 0 fiber), 27g pro. **Diabetic exchanges:** 4 lean meat, 1 starch.

CARIBBEAN CHUTNEY-CRUSTED CHOPS

I like to impress my guests with delicious meals, and these lamb chops are one of my best entrees. It all started with a jar of chutney I received in a gift basket and didn't know what to do with. Folks think I fuss all day over these sophisticated chops, but they're done in only 30 minutes—and they are simply fabulous!

—Josephine Piro, Easton, PA

Takes: 30 min.
Makes: 4 servings

- 1 cup soft bread crumbs
- 1½ tsp. Caribbean jerk seasoning
- ¼ cup mango chutney
- ½ tsp. salt
- ½ tsp. pepper
- 4 lamb loin chops (2 in.-thick and 8 oz. each)

1. Preheat oven to 450°. In a shallow bowl, combine bread crumbs and jerk seasoning; set aside. Combine the chutney, salt and pepper; spread over both sides of lamb chops. Coat with crumb mixture.

2. Place the lamb chops on a rack coated with cooking spray in a shallow baking pan. Bake 20-25 minutes or until meat reaches desired doneness (for medium-rare, a thermometer should read 135°; medium 140°; medium-well, 145°).

1 lamb chop: 296 cal., 10g fat (3g sat. fat), 91mg chol., 711mg sod., 20g carb. (9g sugars, 0 fiber), 30g pro. **Diabetic exchanges:** 4 lean meat, 1 starch.

CARIBBEAN CHUTNEY-CRUSTED CHOPS

KIELBASA SKILLET

I created this meal by accident one day and have been making it ever since. It's also great if you're on a budget.

—Christine Gomez, Corona, CA

Takes: 25 min.
Makes: 2 servings

- ½ lb. smoked kielbasa or Polish sausage, sliced
- 1 cup frozen French-style green beans, thawed
- ½ cup sliced fresh mushrooms
- 1 Tbsp. reduced-sodium soy sauce
- 1 cup hot cooked rice

In a large skillet coated with cooking spray, saute kielbasa until browned. Add the beans, mushrooms and soy sauce; saute 4-5 minutes longer or until vegetables are tender. Serve with rice.

1 serving: 279 cal., 7g fat (2g sat. fat), 71mg chol., 1421mg sod., 31g carb. (5g sugars, 2g fiber), 23g pro.

HAM & BEAN STEW

HAM & BEAN STEW

You only need five ingredients to fix this thick and flavorful stew. It's so easy to make and always a favorite with my family. I top bowls of it with a sprinkling of shredded cheese.
—Teresa D'Amato, East Granby, CT

Prep: 5 min. • **Cook:** 7 hours
Makes: 6 servings

- 2 cans (16 oz. each) baked beans
- 2 medium potatoes, peeled and cubed
- 2 cups cubed fully cooked ham
- 1 celery rib, chopped
- ½ cup water

In a 3-qt. slow cooker, combine all ingredients; mix well. Cover and cook on low for 7 hours or until the potatoes are tender.

1 cup: 213 cal., 5g fat (2g sat. fat), 30mg chol., 919mg sod., 29g carb. (6g sugars, 5g fiber), 14g pro.

GRILLED CURRY PORK CHOPS
WITH APRICOT SAUCE

GRILLED CURRY PORK CHOPS WITH APRICOT SAUCE

A little curry powder and a pinch of cilantro take this tasty flavor combo—pork chops with apricots—in a whole new direction. The recipe's so easy and fantastic, you are sure to get frequent requests for this recipe.

—Julie Hanson, Charleston, ME

Takes: 25 min.
Makes: 4 servings

- 1/4 cup apricot preserves
- 2 tsp. curry powder
- 4 bone-in pork loin chops (3/4 in. thick and 7 oz. each)

SAUCE

- 1 cup canned apricot halves, chopped
- 2 Tbsp. apricot preserves
- 2 tsp. minced fresh cilantro

1. In a small bowl, mix preserves and curry powder; brush over the pork chops.
2. Place pork chops on a greased grill rack. Grill, covered, over medium heat (or broil 4 in. from the heat) 8-10 minutes or until a thermometer reads 145°, turning occasionally. Let rest 5 minutes before serving.
3. Meanwhile, in a small bowl, mix sauce ingredients. Serve with the pork chops.

1 pork chop with 3 Tbsp. sauce: 334 cal., 9g fat (3g sat. fat), 86mg chol., 78mg sod., 34g carb. (24g sugars, 1g fiber), 31g pro.

RANCH PORK ROAST

RANCH PORK ROAST

This simple pork roast with a mild rub is perfect for new cooks. The leftover meat is tender and flavorful enough to be used in countless recipes.
—*Taste of Home* Test Kitchen

Prep: 10 min.
Bake: 50 min. + standing
Makes: 8 servings

- 1 boneless pork loin roast (2½ lbs.)
- 2 Tbsp. olive oil
- 1 Tbsp. ranch salad dressing mix
- 2 tsp. Dijon mustard
- 1 garlic clove, minced
- ½ tsp. pepper

1. Preheat oven to 350°. If desired, tie pork with kitchen string at 2-in. intervals to help roast hold its shape. Combine the next 5 ingredients; rub over the roast. Place on a rack in a shallow roasting pan. Pour 1 cup water into pan.
2. Bake pork roast, uncovered, until a thermometer reads 145°, 50-55 minutes. Let stand for 10-15 minutes before slicing.
Freeze option: Freeze cooled sliced pork in freezer containers. To use, partially thaw pork in refrigerator overnight. Heat through in a covered saucepan, gently stirring; add broth or water if necessary.
4 oz. cooked pork: 212 cal., 10g fat (3g sat. fat), 70mg chol., 248mg sod., 2g carb. (0 sugars, 0 fiber), 27g pro. **Diabetic exchanges:** 4 lean meat, ½ fat.

SECRET'S IN THE SAUCE BBQ RIBS

SECRET'S IN THE SAUCE BBQ RIBS

A sweet, rich sauce makes these ribs so tender that the meat literally falls off the bones. And the aroma is wonderful. Yum!
—Tanya Reid, Winston-Salem, NC

Prep: 10 min. • **Cook:** 6 hours
Makes: 5 servings

- 4½ lbs. pork baby back ribs
- 1½ tsp. pepper
- 2½ cups barbecue sauce
- ¾ cup cherry preserves
- 1 Tbsp. Dijon mustard
- 1 garlic clove, minced

Cut pork ribs into serving-sized pieces; sprinkle with pepper. Place in a 5- or 6-qt. slow cooker. Combine the barbecue sauce, preserves, mustard and garlic; pour over ribs. Cook, covered, on low 6-8 hours or until meat is tender. Serve with sauce.
1 serving: 921 cal., 58g fat (21g sat. fat), 220mg chol., 1402mg sod., 50g carb. (45g sugars, 2g fiber), 48g pro.

SKEWERED LAMB WITH BLACKBERRY-BALSAMIC GLAZE

Lamb instantly makes things more special. This dish proves it takes only a few quality ingredients to make a classy main dish.

—Elynor "Elly" Townsend, Summerfield, WI

Prep: 10 min. + marinating
Grill: 10 min. • **Makes:** 6 servings

- ½ cup seedless blackberry spreadable fruit
- ⅓ cup balsamic vinegar
- 1 Tbsp. minced fresh rosemary or 1 tsp. dried rosemary, crushed
- 1 Tbsp. Dijon mustard
- 1½ lbs. lean boneless lamb, cut into 1-in. cubes
- ¼ tsp. salt

1. In a small bowl, combine the spreadable fruit, vinegar, rosemary and mustard. Pour ⅔ cup marinade into a shallow dish; add lamb. Turn to coat; cover and refrigerate for at least 1 hour. Cover and refrigerate remaining marinade for basting.

2. Drain lamb, discarding marinade in dish. Thread lamb onto 6 metal or soaked wooden skewers. Place kabobs on a greased grill rack. Grill, covered, over medium heat (or broil 4 in. from the heat) until lamb reaches desired doneness (for medium-rare, a thermometer should read 135°; medium, 140°; medium-well, 145°), 10-12 minutes, turning once and basting frequently with reserved marinade. Sprinkle with salt before serving.

1 kabob: 255 cal., 9g fat (4g sat. fat), 103mg chol., 264mg sod., 9g carb. (7g sugars, 0 fiber), 32g pro. **Diabetic exchanges:** 5 lean meat, ½ starch.

SKEWERED LAMB WITH BLACKBERRY-BALSAMIC GLAZE

PEPPERED PORK WITH MUSHROOM SAUCE

PEPPERED PORK WITH MUSHROOM SAUCE

Using pre-seasoned pork tenderloin gives us flavorful, quick and satisfying meals without a big mess or leftovers. I have used all flavors of pork tenderloin for this recipe.
—Jolene Roszel, Helena, MT

Takes: 30 min.
Makes: 4 servings

- 2 Tbsp. olive oil, divided
- 1 peppercorn pork tenderloin (1 lb.) or flavor of your choice, cut into ¾-in. slices
- ½ cup sliced fresh mushrooms
- ¼ cup chopped onion
- 2 Tbsp. all-purpose flour
- 1 cup reduced-sodium beef broth

1. In a large skillet, heat 1 Tbsp. oil over medium heat. Brown the pork on both sides. Remove pork from pan.
2. In same pan, heat remaining oil over medium-high heat. Add mushrooms and onion; cook and stir until tender, 4-5 minutes.
3. In a small bowl, mix flour and broth until smooth. Stir into mushroom mixture. Bring to a boil; cook and stir until sauce is thickened. Return pork to pan. Cook until a thermometer inserted in pork reads 145°.

3 oz. cooked pork with ¼ cup sauce: 208 cal., 11g fat (2g sat. fat), 55mg chol., 785mg sod., 7g carb. (1g sugars, 0 fiber), 21g pro.

TEST KITCHEN TIP
Pre-marinated pork tenderloin makes easy work of weeknight dinners. Flavors vary by grocery store, but this versatile sauce will complement nearly any variety.

SPAGHETTI SQUASH & SAUSAGE EASY MEAL

SPAGHETTI SQUASH & SAUSAGE EASY MEAL

My son's favorite dish simply uses homegrown spaghetti squash, kielbasa, and pico de gallo or salsa. Easy, fast and oh-so-tasty.

—Pam Mascarenas, Taylorsville, UT

Takes: 30 min.
Makes: 6 servings

- 1 medium spaghetti squash
- 1 Tbsp. olive oil
- 1 pkg. (14 oz.) smoked sausage, halved lengthwise and sliced
- 1 cup pico de gallo
- ¼ tsp. salt
- ⅛ tsp. pepper

1. Cut the squash lengthwise in half; discard seeds. Place the halves on a microwave-safe plate, cut side down. Microwave, uncovered, on high until tender, 15-20 minutes.

2. Meanwhile, in a large skillet, heat the oil over medium heat. Add the sausage; cook and stir 4-5 minutes or until sausage is lightly browned.

3. When the spaghetti squash is cool enough to handle, use a fork to separate strands. Add squash, pico de gallo, salt and pepper to sausage; heat through, tossing to combine.

1 cups: 326 cal., 22g fat (8g sat. fat), 44mg chol., 901mg sod., 24g carb. (2g sugars, 5g fiber), 12g pro.

TEST KITCHEN TIP
Eating fewer carbs but still want a hearty and satisfying dinner? One cup of cooked spaghetti squash has roughly 10 grams carbs, versus 45 grams for regular spaghetti pasta.

GRILLED DIJON PORK ROAST

I came up with this recipe one day after not having much in the house to eat. My husband loved it, and it has become the only way I make pork now.
—Cyndi Lacy-Andersen, Woodinville, WA

Prep: 10 min. + marinating
Grill: 1 hour + standing
Makes: 12 servings

- ⅓ cup balsamic vinegar
- 3 Tbsp. Dijon mustard
- 1 Tbsp. honey
- 1 tsp. salt
- 1 boneless pork loin roast (3 to 4 lbs.)

1. In a bowl or shallow dish, whisk vinegar, mustard, honey and salt. Add pork; turn to coat. Cover and refrigerate at least 8 hours or overnight.
2. Prepare grill for indirect heat, using a drip pan.
3. Drain the pork, discarding marinade. Place the pork on a greased grill rack over drip pan and cook, covered, over indirect medium heat for 1-1½ hours or until a thermometer reads 145°, turning occasionally. Let stand 10 minutes before slicing.

3 oz. cooked pork: 149 cal., 5g fat (2g sat. fat), 56mg chol., 213mg sod., 2g carb. (1g sugars, 0 fiber), 22g pro. **Diabetic exchanges:** 3 lean meat.

GRILLED DIJON PORK ROAST

ROSEMARY-THYME LAMB CHOPS

My father loves lamb, so I make this dish whenever he visits. It's the perfect main course for holidays or get-togethers.

—Kristina Mitchell, Clearwater, FL

Takes: 30 min.
Makes: 4 servings

- 8 lamb loin chops (3 oz. each)
- ½ tsp. pepper
- ¼ tsp. salt
- 3 Tbsp. Dijon mustard
- 1 Tbsp. minced fresh rosemary
- 1 Tbsp. minced fresh thyme
- 3 garlic cloves, minced

1. Sprinkle lamb chops with pepper and salt. In a small bowl, mix mustard, rosemary, thyme and garlic.

2. Grill chops, covered, on an oiled rack over medium heat 6 minutes. Turn; spread herb mixture over chops. Grill lamb 6-8 minutes longer or until meat reaches desired doneness (for medium-rare, a thermometer should read 135°; medium, 140°; medium-well, 145°).

2 lamb chops: 231 cal., 9g fat (4g sat. fat), 97mg chol., 493mg sod., 3g carb. (0 sugars, 0 fiber), 32g pro. **Diabetic Exchange:** 4 lean meat.

ANDOUILLE-STUFFED PEPPERS

I was inspired by the important role of green peppers in Cajun dishes when I created my spiced-up recipe. For a healthier choice, substitute chicken sausage or cubed cooked chicken breast for the andouille sausage.

—Sarah Larson, Carlsbad, CA

Prep: 40 min. • **Bake:** 40 min.
Makes: 4 servings

- 1 pkg. (8 oz.) jambalaya mix
- 4 small green peppers
- ¾ lb. fully cooked andouille sausage links, chopped
- 1 jalapeno pepper, seeded and minced
- 1 can (16 oz.) tomato juice
- Louisiana-style hot sauce, optional

1. Prepare the jambalaya mix according to package directions. Meanwhile, cut the peppers lengthwise in half; remove the seeds.

2. In a large skillet, cook and stir sausage over medium-high heat until browned. Add jalapeno; cook 1 minute longer.

3. Stir sausage mixture into prepared jambalaya. Spoon into green pepper halves. Place in a greased 13x9-in. baking dish; pour the tomato juice over and around peppers.

4. Bake, uncovered, at 350° for 40-45 minutes or until peppers are tender. Serve with hot sauce if desired.

1 stuffed pepper: 443 cal., 17g fat (6g sat. fat), 110mg chol., 1935mg sod., 54g carb. (5g sugars, 2g fiber), 23g pro.

ROSEMARY-THYME
LAMB CHOPS

HAM & ZUCCHINI ITALIANO

HAM & ZUCCHINI ITALIANO

I strongly believe dinner should be these three things: healthy, delicious and simple. With fresh zucchini, deli ham and marinara sauce baked with mozzarella cheese, you can accomplish all three in the time it takes to describe the dish.
—Madison Mayberry, Ames, IA

Takes: 30 min.
Makes: 4 servings

- 3 medium zucchini, cut diagonally into ¼-in. slices
- 1 Tbsp. olive oil
- 1 tsp. dried basil
- ½ tsp. salt
- ¼ tsp. pepper
- ½ lb. smoked deli ham, cut into strips
- 1 cup marinara or spaghetti sauce
- ¾ cup shredded part-skim mozzarella cheese

1. Preheat oven to 450°. In a large skillet, saute the zucchini in oil until crisp-tender. Sprinkle zucchini with the basil, salt and pepper.
2. Place half of the zucchini in a greased 8-in. square baking dish. Layer with half of the ham, marinara sauce and cheese. Repeat layers.
3. Bake, uncovered, until heated through and cheese is melted, 10-12 minutes. Serve with a slotted spoon.

1 serving: 196 cal., 8g fat (3g sat. fat), 36mg chol., 1013mg sod., 14g carb. (9g sugars, 3g fiber), 17g pro.

MAPLE-PEACH GLAZED HAM

This is one of my husband's favorite recipes. He makes it regularly for his group of friends on the weekends because it's so good and easy.
—Bonnie Hawkins, Elkhorn, WI

Prep: 5 min. • **Bake:** 2 hours
Makes: 16 servings (about 2 cups sauce)

- 1 fully cooked bone-in ham (7 to 9 lbs.)
- 2 cups peach preserves or orange marmalade
- ½ cup maple syrup
- ⅓ cup orange juice
- 2 Tbsp. ground ancho chile pepper, optional

1. Preheat oven to 325°. Place the ham on a rack in a shallow roasting pan. Cover and bake until a thermometer reads 130°, 1¾-2¼ hours.

2. Meanwhile, in a saucepan, mix preserves, syrup, orange juice and, if desired, chili pepper until blended. Remove ¾ cup mixture for glaze.

3. Remove ham from oven; brush with some of the glaze. Bake, uncovered, 15-20 minutes longer or until a thermometer reads 140°, brushing occasionally with remaining glaze.

4. In a saucepan over medium heat, bring preserves mixture to a boil, stirring occasionally. Cook and stir until slightly thickened, 1-2 minutes. Serve as a sauce with ham.

4 oz. cooked ham with 2 Tbsp. sauce: 294 cal., 5g fat (2g sat. fat), 87mg chol., 1040mg sod., 34g carb. (31g sugars, 0 fiber), 29g pro.

MAPLE-PEACH GLAZED HAM

TEST KITCHEN TIP
Remember this peach-citrus sauce. It is great to brush over cooked chicken and pork chops when looking for a quick and easy way to dress up weeknight dinners.

TAILGATE SAUSAGES

TAILGATE SAUSAGES

You'll need just a handful of ingredients to fix these tasty sandwiches. Fully cooked sausages are placed in buns with cheese and topped with giardiniera, then wrapped in foil so they're easy to transport and a breeze to grill.

—Matthew Hass, Ellison Bay, WI

Takes: 20 min.
Makes: 4 servings

- ½ cup giardiniera, drained
- ½ tsp. sugar
- 4 slices provolone cheese
- 4 brat buns or hot dog buns, split
- 4 cooked Italian sausage links
- Additional giardiniera, optional

1. In a bowl, combine giardiniera and sugar; set aside.
2. Place cheese in buns; top with sausages and giardiniera mixture. Wrap individually in a double thickness of heavy-duty foil (about 12x10 in.). Grill, uncovered, over medium heat for 8-10 minutes or until heated through and cheese is melted. Open foil carefully to allow steam to escape. If desired, serve the sausages with additional giardiniera.

1 sausage: 584 cal., 33g fat (15g sat. fat), 84mg chol., 1401mg sod., 39g carb. (9g sugars, 2g fiber), 31g pro.

ITALIAN-STYLE PORK CHOPS

An Italian-style version of pork chops was one of the first recipes I tried making in the early years of my marriage. I've changed it over the years to be healthier by reducing added oil and fat and adding in some vegetables. It's great served over hot rice.

—Traci Hoppes, Spring Valley, CA

Takes: 30 min.
Makes: 4 servings

- 2 medium green peppers, cut into ¼-in. strips
- ½ lb. sliced fresh mushrooms
- 1 Tbsp. plus 1½ tsp. olive oil, divided
- 4 boneless pork loin chops (6 oz. each)
- ¾ tsp. salt, divided
- ¾ tsp. pepper, divided
- 2 cups marinara or spaghetti sauce
- 1 can (3½ oz.) sliced ripe olives, drained

1. In a skillet, saute peppers and mushrooms in 1 Tbsp. oil until tender. Remove and keep warm.

2. Sprinkle the pork chops with ¼ tsp. salt and ¼ tsp. pepper. In the same skillet, brown chops in remaining oil. Add the marinara sauce, olives, remaining salt and pepper, and reserved pepper mixture. Bring to a boil. Reduce heat; cover and simmer until a thermometer inserted in the pork reads 145°, 10-15 minutes. Let pork stand for 5 minutes before serving.

1 pork chop with ¾ cup sauce: 397 cal., 18g fat (5g sat. fat), 82mg chol., 930mg sod., 22g carb. (12g sugars, 5g fiber), 37g pro.

ROAST LEG OF LAMB

ROAST LEG OF LAMB

Lamb intimidates some, but this recipe uses a simple herb mixture that always provides a ton of flavor.
—Sharon Cusson, Augusta, ME

Prep: 5 min.
Bake: 2 hours + standing
Makes: 10 servings

- 1 bone-in leg of lamb (6 to 8 lbs.), trimmed
- 2 garlic cloves, minced
- ½ tsp. dried thyme
- ½ tsp. dried marjoram
- ½ tsp. dried oregano
- ¼ tsp. salt
- ⅛ tsp. pepper
- 1 tsp. canola oil

1. Preheat oven to 325°. Place lamb on a rack in a shallow roasting pan, fat side up. Cut 12-14 slits ½ in. deep in roast. Combine garlic, thyme, marjoram, oregano, salt and pepper; spoon 2 tsp. into the slits. Brush roast with oil; rub with remaining herb mixture.
2. Bake, uncovered, until meat reaches desired doneness (for medium-rare, a thermometer should read 135°; medium, 140°; medium-well, 145°), 2-2½ hours. Let leg of lamb stand at least 15 minutes before slicing.

5 oz. cooked lamb: 227 cal., 9g fat (4g sat. fat), 122mg chol., 114mg sod., 0 carb. (0 sugars, 0 fiber), 34g pro. **Diabetic exchanges:** 5 lean meat.

PORCINI-CRUSTED PORK WITH POLENTA

PORCINI-CRUSTED PORK WITH POLENTA

Rosemary and Parmesan meet earthy mushroom undertones in this restaurant-quality dish you can proudly call your own.
—Casandra Rittenhouse, North Hollywood, CA

Prep: 20 min.
Bake: 20 min. • **Makes:** 4 servings

- 1 pkg. (1 oz.) dried porcini mushrooms
- ¼ tsp. salt
- ¼ tsp. pepper
- 4 bone-in pork loin chops (7 oz. each)
- 2 tsp. olive oil
- 1 tube (1 lb.) polenta
- ½ cup grated Parmesan cheese
- ¼ tsp. dried rosemary, crushed

1. Preheat oven to 375°. Process the mushrooms in a food processor until coarsely chopped. Transfer to a shallow bowl; stir in salt and pepper. Press 1 side of each pork chop into the mushroom mixture.
2. In a large cast-iron or other ovenproof skillet, heat oil over medium-high heat. Place chops, mushroom side down, in skillet; cook 2 minutes on each side. Bake, uncovered, 20-25 minutes or until a thermometer inserted in pork reads 145°. Let stand 5 minutes before serving.
3. Prepare polenta according to package directions for soft polenta. Stir in cheese and rosemary. Serve with pork.

1 serving: 397 cal., 14g fat (5g sat. fat), 94mg chol., 825mg sod., 26g carb. (2g sugars, 3g fiber), 38 g pro.

TUSCAN GRAPES & SAUSAGES

This is a recipe that is always a go-to when entertaining. It is simple and elegant, and you can be with your guests instead of spending the entire time in the kitchen. It is always a crowd-pleaser and everyone asks for the recipe. I serve this over rustic hand-mashed red potatoes. I love the pieces of garlic in this dish because they become so sweet—a nice complement to the sweet grapes and spicy sausage.
—Melissa Zienter, Las Vegas, NV

Prep: 30 min. • **Bake:** 15 min.
Makes: 8 servings

- 8 uncooked Italian sausage links (4 oz. each), hot or mild
- 2½ lbs. seedless green or red grapes, or a mixture
- 20 to 30 garlic cloves, peeled and halved
- ½ cup butter, divided
- ¼ cup balsamic vinegar

1. Preheat oven to 450°. Place sausage links in a saucepan; add water to cover. Bring to a boil. Reduce heat; simmer, covered, until sausages are no longer pink and some fat has been rendered, 20-25 minutes. Drain. When cool enough to handle, cut into ½-in. slices.
2. Meanwhile, remove grape stems; place grapes and garlic in a 15x10x1-in. baking pan. Melt 6 Tbsp. butter; drizzle over grapes and garlic. Toss to coat. Top with sausage slices. Bake until the sausage is browned, 15-20 minutes, stirring once.
3. Using a slotted spoon, transfer sausage mixture to a serving dish. Keep warm. Transfer cooking juices to a small saucepan; add balsamic vinegar. Bring to a boil. Cook until liquid is reduced by half, 4-5 minutes. Remove from the heat. Stir in remaining 2 Tbsp. butter, 1 Tbsp. at a time, until melted. Drizzle over sausage and grapes.

1½ cups: 498 cal., 36g fat (15g sat. fat), 92mg chol., 799mg sod., 32g carb. (25g sugars, 1g fiber), 13g pro.

★★★★★ **READER REVIEW**
"The roasted garlic with the butter and grapes make this really good if you love garlic (and who doesn't?). You might want to make it for Friday dinner, though, or your co-workers may keep their distance from you the next day."
—WHEELER, TASTEOFHOME.COM

TUSCAN GRAPES & SAUSAGES

CIDER-GLAZED PORK TENDERLOIN

This is a super easy recipe full of sweet fall flavor. The maple taste really shines through.
—Susan Stetzel, Gainesville, NY

Takes: 30 min.
Makes: 4 servings

- 1 pork tenderloin (1 lb.)
- ¼ tsp. salt
- ½ tsp. pepper, divided
- 1 Tbsp. olive oil
- ¾ cup apple cider or juice
- ¼ cup maple syrup
- 2 Tbsp. cider vinegar

1. Preheat oven to 425°. Cut the tenderloin in half to fit skillet; sprinkle with salt and ¼ tsp. pepper. In a large skillet, heat the oil over medium-high heat; brown the pork on all sides. Transfer to a 15x10x1-in. pan. Roast until a thermometer reads 145°, 12-15 minutes.

2. Meanwhile, in same skillet, bring the cider, syrup, vinegar and remaining pepper to a boil, stirring to loosen browned bits from pan. Cook, uncovered, until mixture is reduced to a glaze consistency, about 5 minutes.

3. Remove pork from oven; let stand 5 minutes before slicing. Serve with glaze.

3 oz. cooked pork with 1 Tbsp. glaze: 239 cal., 7g fat (2g sat. fat), 64mg chol., 200mg sod., 19g carb. (17g sugars, 0 fiber), 23g pro.
Diabetic exchanges: 3 lean meat, 1 starch, 1 fat.

ROSEMARY-APRICOT PORK TENDERLOIN

ROSEMARY-APRICOT PORK TENDERLOIN

You'll be surprised at how fast this dish comes together for an easy weeknight meal. And with very little effort, you'll have tender and juicy meat that just begs to be added to a salad or sandwich the next day.

—Marie Rizzio, Interlochen, MI

Prep: 15 min. • **Bake:** 25 min.
Makes: 8 servings

- 3 Tbsp. minced fresh rosemary or 1 Tbsp. dried rosemary, crushed
- 3 Tbsp. olive oil, divided
- 4 garlic cloves, minced
- 1 tsp. salt
- ½ tsp. pepper
- 2 pork tenderloins (1 lb. each)

GLAZE

- 1 cup apricot preserves
- 3 Tbsp. lemon juice
- 2 garlic cloves, minced

1. In a small bowl, combine the rosemary, 1 Tbsp. oil, garlic, salt and pepper; brush over pork.
2. In a large cast-iron or other ovenproof skillet, brown pork in remaining oil on all sides. Bake at 425° for 15 minutes.
3. In a small bowl, combine the glaze ingredients; brush over pork. Bake until a thermometer reads 145°, basting occasionally with pan juices, 10-15 minutes longer. Let stand for 5 minutes before slicing.

3 oz. cooked pork: 280 cal., 9g fat (2g sat. fat), 63mg chol., 357mg sod., 27g carb. (15g sugars, 0 fiber), 23g pro.

PRESSURE-COOKED MESQUITE RIBS

When we're missing the grill during winter, these tangy ribs give us that same smoky barbecue taste we love. They are so simple, and fall-off-the-bone delicious, too!

—Sue Evans, Marquette, MI

Prep: 15 min.
Cook: 40 min. + releasing
Makes: 8 servings

- 1 cup water
- 2 Tbsp. cider vinegar
- 1 Tbsp. soy sauce
- 4 lbs. pork baby back ribs, cut into serving-sized portions
- 2 Tbsp. mesquite seasoning
- ¾ cup barbecue sauce, divided

1. Combine water, vinegar and soy sauce in a 6-qt. electric pressure cooker. Rub the pork ribs with mesquite seasoning; add to pressure cooker. Lock lid; close pressure-release valve. Adjust to pressure-cook on high for 35 minutes. Let pressure naturally release for 10 minutes, then quick-release any pressure that remains.

2. Remove ribs to a foil-lined baking sheet. Preheat broiler. Brush ribs with half the barbecue sauce. Broil 4-6 in. from heat 2-4 minutes or until glazed. Brush with remaining barbecue sauce.

1 serving: 329 cal., 21g fat (8g sat. fat), 81mg chol., 678mg sod., 10g carb. (8g sugars, 0 fiber), 23g pro.

PRESSURE-COOKED MESQUITE RIBS

FISH & SEAFOOD

PESTO CORN SALAD WITH SHRIMP
P. 152

1 2 3 4 5

IT'S EASY TO JAZZ UP A MAIN COURSE WHEN SEAFOOD IS THE STAR OF THE SHOW!

CILANTRO-TOPPED SALMON

CILANTRO-TOPPED SALMON

This has been a favorite with everyone who has tried it. A tongue-tingling cilantro-lime sauce complements tender salmon fillets in the very pleasing entree.
—Nancy Culbert, Whitehorn, CA

Takes: 30 min.
Makes: 6 servings

- 1½ lbs. salmon fillets
- ¼ cup lime juice, divided
- ½ cup minced fresh cilantro
- 3 Tbsp. thinly sliced green onions
- 1 Tbsp. finely chopped jalapeno pepper
- 1 Tbsp. olive oil
- ¼ tsp. salt
- ⅛ tsp. pepper
- Optional: lime wedge, sliced jalapeno and cilantro sprigs

1. Preheat oven to 350°. Place the salmon skin side down in a 13x9-in. baking dish coated with cooking spray. Drizzle with 1½ tsp. lime juice.
2. In a small bowl, combine the cilantro, onions, jalapeno, oil, salt, pepper and remaining lime juice. Spread over salmon. Bake, uncovered, until the fish just begins to flakes easily with a fork, 20-25 minutes. If desired, serve with lime wedges, sliced jalapeno and cilantro sprigs.
3 oz.-weight: 232 cal., 15g fat (3g sat. fat), 67mg chol., 166mg sod., 1g carb. (0 sugars, 0 fiber), 23g pro. **Diabetic exchanges:** 3 lean meat, 1 fat.

LIME-MARINATED ORANGE ROUGHY

LIME-MARINATED ORANGE ROUGHY

This dish is simple, flavorful and not fattening at all. And because it's so quick, you can have company over and spend all your time visiting.
—Pam Corder, Monroe, LA

Prep: 10 min. + marinating
Broil: 10 min. • **Makes:** 4 servings

- 4 orange roughy fillets (6 oz. each)
- ⅓ cup water
- ⅓ cup lime juice
- 2 Tbsp. honey
- 1 Tbsp. canola oil
- ½ tsp. dill weed

1. Place fillets in a 13x9-in. baking dish. In a small bowl, whisk remaining ingredients until blended. Pour ½ cup marinade over fillets; turn to coat. Refrigerate 1 hour. Cover and refrigerate the remaining marinade.
2. Preheat broiler. Drain fish, discarding marinade in dish. Place fish on a broiler pan coated with cooking spray. Broil 4-6 in. from heat until fish just begins to flake easily with a fork, 4-6 minutes on each side, basting frequently with the reserved marinade.
1 serving: 169 cal., 3g fat (0 sat. fat), 102mg chol., 123mg sod., 6g carb. (5g sugars, 0 fiber), 28g pro. **Diabetic exchanges:** 4 lean meat, ½ starch, ½ fat.

PARMESAN FISH FILLETS

The hint of Parmesan cheese really seals the deal for this tilapia recipe. It's fast, a cinch to make and good for you, too!
—Paula Alf, Sharonville, OH

Takes: 30 min.
Makes: 2 servings

- ¼ cup egg substitute
- 1 Tbsp. fat-free milk
- ⅓ cup grated Parmesan cheese
- 2 Tbsp. all-purpose flour
- 2 tilapia fillets (5 oz. each)

1. In a shallow bowl, combine egg substitute and milk. In another shallow bowl, combine cheese and flour. Dip fillets in egg mixture, then coat with cheese mixture.
2. Place on a baking sheet coated with cooking spray. Bake at 350° until fish flakes easily with a fork, 20-25 minutes.

1 piece: 196 cal., 5g fat (3g sat. fat), 78mg chol., 279mg sod., 5g carb. (1g sugars, 0 fiber), 33g pro. **Diabetic exchanges:** 4 lean meat.

TEST KITCHEN TIP
It's easy to jazz up this dish without adding fat. Simply mix a dash of basil, oregano, rosemary, thyme or even Italian seasoning into the flour-Parmesan cheese mixture.

CREOLE BAKED TILAPIA

Because I'm originally from Louisiana, I love Creole cooking. Something as simple as adding a spice blend can go a long way to improving a basic fish bake.
—Carolyn Collins, Freeport, TX

Takes: 25 min.
Makes: 4 servings

- 4 tilapia fillets (6 oz. each)
- 1 can (8 oz.) tomato sauce
- 1 small green pepper, thinly sliced
- ½ cup chopped red onion
- 1 tsp. Creole seasoning

1. Preheat oven to 350°. Place tilapia in an ungreased 13x9-in. baking dish. In a small bowl, combine tomato sauce, green pepper, onion and Creole seasoning; pour over the fillets.
2. Bake, uncovered, until fish flakes easily with a fork, 20-25 minutes.

1 serving: 166 cal., 2g fat (1g sat. fat), 83mg chol., 488mg sod., 6g carb. (2g sugars, 1g fiber), 33g pro. **Diabetic exchanges:** 5 lean meat, 1 vegetable.

CREOLE BAKED TILAPIA

PESTO FISH
WITH PINE NUTS

PESTO FISH WITH PINE NUTS

I love fish, and Italian flavors are my favorite. This is a tasty way to get more healthy fish into your diet.

—Valery Anderson,
Sterling Heights, MI

Takes: 15 min.
Makes: 4 servings

- 2 envelopes pesto sauce mix, divided
- 4 cod fillets (6 oz. each)
- ¼ cup olive oil
- ½ cup shredded Parmesan or Romano cheese
- ½ cup pine nuts, toasted

1. Prepare 1 envelope pesto sauce mix according to package directions. Sprinkle fillets with remaining pesto mix, patting to help adhere.
2. In a large skillet, heat oil over medium heat. Add fillets; cook until fish just begins to flake easily with a fork, 4-5 minutes on each side. Remove from heat. Sprinkle with cheese and pine nuts. Serve with pesto sauce.

1 fillet with scant 3 Tbsp. pesto sauce: 560 cal., 39g fat (5g sat. fat), 72mg chol., 1522mg sod., 17g carb. (7g sugars, 1g fiber), 35g pro.

Pesto Chicken with Pine Nuts: Substitute 4 boneless skinless chicken breasts (6 oz. each) for the cod. Cook until a thermometer reads 165°, 6-8 minutes on each side.

CAESAR ORANGE ROUGHY

CAESAR ORANGE ROUGHY

I'm so thankful that my mother, a fantastic cook, taught me the ropes in the kitchen when I was fairly young. Mom won several cooking contests over the years, and this is one of my favorite recipes of hers.

—Mary Lou Boyce, Wilmington, DE

Takes: 25 min.
Makes: 8 servings

- 8 orange roughy fillets (4 oz. each)
- 1 cup creamy Caesar salad dressing
- 2 cups crushed butter-flavored crackers (about 50 crackers)
- 1 cup shredded cheddar cheese

1. Preheat oven to 400°. Place the orange roughy fillets in an ungreased 13x9-in. baking dish. Drizzle with the salad dressing; sprinkle with the crushed crackers.
2. Bake, uncovered, 10 minutes. Sprinkle with cheese. Bake until fish flakes easily with a fork and cheese is melted, 3-5 minutes longer.

1 serving: 421 cal., 28g fat (6g sat. fat), 93mg chol., 716mg sod., 17g carb. (3g sugars, 1g fiber), 24g pro.

SKEWERED GINGER SHRIMP WITH PLUMS

Sweet, simple and sensational, these shrimp skewers boast loads of flavor with just four ingredients. Throw them on the grill for a quick dinner or a tasty potluck dish.

—*Taste of Home* Test Kitchen

Takes: 25 min.
Makes: 4 servings

- 1 lb. uncooked large shrimp, peeled and deveined
- 2 medium plums or peaches, cut into wedges
- ½ cup sesame ginger marinade, divided
- 1 green onion, thinly sliced
- Optional: Sesame seeds and lime wedges

1. In a large bowl, combine the shrimp and plums. Drizzle with ¼ cup marinade; toss to coat. Alternately thread shrimp and plums on 4 metal or soaked wooden skewers.
2. On a lightly oiled rack, grill skewers, covered, over medium heat or broil 4 in. from heat until shrimp turn pink, 6-8 minutes, turning occasionally and basting frequently with the remaining ¼ cup marinade during the last 3 minutes of cooking. Serve with green onion and, if desired, sesame seeds and lime wedges.

1 skewer: 173 cal., 2g fat (0 sat. fat), 138mg chol., 1295mg sod., 19g carb. (15g sugars, 1g fiber), 19g pro.

SKEWERED GINGER SHRIMP WITH PLUMS

SCALLOPS IN SAGE CREAM FOR TWO

GRILLED LOBSTER TAILS

I never made lobster at home until I tried this convenient and deliciously different grilled recipe. It turned out amazing, and it has left me with little reason to ever order lobster at a restaurant again.

—Katie Rush, Kansas City, MO

Prep: 15 min. + marinating
Grill: 10 min. • **Makes:** 6 servings

- 6 frozen lobster tails (8 to 10 oz. each), thawed
- ¾ cup olive oil
- 3 Tbsp. minced fresh chives
- 3 garlic cloves, minced
- ½ tsp. salt
- ½ tsp. pepper

1. Using scissors, cut 3 to 4 lengthwise slits in underside of each tail to loosen the shell slightly. Cut top of lobster shell lengthwise down the center with scissors, leaving tail fin intact. Cut shell at an angle away from center of tail at base of the tail fin. Loosen meat from shell, keeping the fin end attached; lift meat and lay over the shell.
2. In a small bowl, combine the remaining ingredients; spoon over lobster meat. Cover and refrigerate for 20 minutes.
3. Place lobster tails, meat side up, on grill rack. Grill, covered, over medium heat until meat is opaque, 10-12 minutes.

1 lobster tail: 446 cal., 29g fat (4g sat. fat), 215mg chol., 869mg sod., 2g carb. (0 sugars, 0 fiber), 43g pro.

SCALLOPS IN SAGE CREAM FOR TWO

I didn't want to hide the ocean freshness of some scallops that I bought on the dock from a local fisherman, so I decided to use simple but perfect ingredients to showcase them.

—Joan Churchill, Dover, NH

Takes: 20 min.
Makes: 2 servings

- ¾ lb. sea scallops
- ⅛ tsp. salt
- Dash pepper
- 2 Tbsp. olive oil, divided
- ¼ cup chopped shallots
- ⅓ cup heavy whipping cream
- 3 fresh sage leaves, thinly sliced
- Hot cooked pasta, optional

1. Sprinkle scallops with salt and pepper. In a large skillet, saute scallops in 1 Tbsp. oil until firm and opaque, 1½-2 minutes on each side. Remove scallops and keep warm.
2. In the same skillet, saute the shallots in remaining 1 Tbsp. oil until tender. Add cream; bring to a boil. Cook and stir until sauce is slightly thickened, about 30 seconds.
3. Return scallops to the pan; heat through. Stir in the sage. Serve with pasta if desired.

1 serving: 421 cal., 29g fat (11g sat. fat), 110mg chol., 439mg sod., 9g carb. (1g sugars, 0 fiber), 30g pro.

GRILLED LOBSTER TAILS

PESTO CORN SALAD WITH SHRIMP

PESTO CORN SALAD WITH SHRIMP

This recipe showcases the beautiful bounty of summer with its fresh corn, tomatoes and delicious basil. Prevent browning by spritzing the salad with lemon juice.
—Deena Bowen, Chico, CA

Takes: 30 min.
Makes: 4 servings

- 4 medium ears sweet corn, husked
- ½ cup packed fresh basil leaves
- ¼ cup olive oil
- ½ tsp. salt, divided
- 1½ cups cherry tomatoes, halved
- ⅛ tsp. pepper
- 1 medium ripe avocado, peeled and chopped
- 1 lb. uncooked shrimp (31-40 per lb.), peeled and deveined

1. In a pot of boiling water, cook the corn until tender, about 5 minutes. Drain; cool slightly. Meanwhile, in a food processor, pulse basil, oil and ¼ tsp. salt until blended.
2. Cut corn from cob and place in a bowl. Stir in tomatoes, pepper and remaining ¼ tsp. salt. Add avocado and 2 Tbsp. basil mixture; toss gently to combine.
3. Thread shrimp onto metal or soaked wooden skewers; brush with remaining basil mixture. Grill, covered, over medium heat until the shrimp turn pink, about 2-4 minutes per side. Remove shrimp from skewers; serve with corn mixture.

1 serving: 371 cal., 22g fat (3g sat. fat), 138mg chol., 450mg sod., 25g carb. (8g sugars, 5g fiber), 23g pro.

AIR-FRYER SESAME-GINGER SALMON

My family likes to eat healthy, and fish is one of our favorite proteins. I try to find different ways to make salmon to help give variety to our meals. This dish is a way to do just that.

—Jennifer Berry, Lexington, OH

Prep: 15 min. + marinating
Cook: 15 min. • **Makes:** 4 servings

- 1 cup sesame ginger salad dressing, divided
- 4 green onions, chopped
- 2 Tbsp. minced fresh cilantro
- 4 salmon fillets (4 oz. each)

1. In a large bowl or shallow dish, combine ⅔ cup dressing, onions and cilantro. Add salmon and turn to coat. Refrigerate for 30 minutes.
2. Preheat air fryer to 375°. Drain salmon, discarding marinade. Place salmon in a single layer on greased tray in air-fryer basket.
3. Cook for 10 minutes. Baste with remaining dressing. Cook until fish flakes easily with a fork, 5-10 minutes. Drizzle with pan juices before serving.

1 fillet: 234 cal., 15g fat (3g sat. fat), 57mg chol., 208mg sod., 4g carb. (3g sugars, 0 fiber), 19g pro.

AIR-FRYER SESAME-GINGER SALMON

BACON HONEY WALLEYE

The texture and flavor of the walleye is only enhanced by this recipe's savory-sweet topping. It takes only a few minutes to grill.

—Linda Neumann, Algonac, MI

Prep: 20 min.
Grill: 15 min. **Makes:** 8 servings

- 16 bacon strips, partially cooked
- 4 walleye fillets (2½ lbs.)
- 1 cup thinly sliced onion
- ¼ cup butter, melted
- 2 Tbsp. honey
- ½ tsp. salt
- ¼ tsp. pepper

1. Fold four 18x15-in. pieces of heavy-duty aluminum foil in half; fold up edges to make pans about 12x7 in. Place 4 strips of bacon in each foil pan; top each with a fillet and ¼ cup onion. Drizzle with the butter and honey. Sprinkle with salt and pepper.
2. Grill, covered, over medium heat until fish flakes easily with a fork, 12-15 minutes. Open foil carefully to allow steam to escape. Cut fillets in half; serve each with 2 bacon strips.

3¾ oz.-weight: 277 cal., 14g fat (6g sat. fat), 148mg chol., 480mg sod., 6g carb. (5g sugars, 0 fiber), 31g pro.

HERB-ROASTED SALMON FILLETS

Roasted salmon is so simple, but it is elegant enough to serve to company. I make it on days when I have less than an hour to cook.

—Luanne Asta, Hampton Bays, NY

Takes: 30 min.
Makes: 4 servings

- 4 salmon fillets (6 oz. each)
- 4 garlic cloves, minced
- 1 Tbsp. minced fresh rosemary or 1 tsp. dried rosemary, crushed
- 1 Tbsp. olive oil
- 2 tsp. minced fresh thyme or ½ tsp. dried thyme
- ¾ tsp. salt
- ½ tsp. pepper

Preheat oven to 425°. Place salmon in a greased 15x10x1-in. baking pan, skin side down. Combine remaining ingredients; spread over fillets. Roast until salmon just beings to flake easily with a fork, 15-18 minutes.

1 fillet: 301 cal., 19g fat (4g sat. fat), 85mg chol., 529mg sod., 1g carb. (0 sugars, 0 fiber), 29g pro.
Diabetic exchanges: 4 lean meat, 1 fat.

TEST KITCHEN TIP
Lining baking pans with parchment always makes cleanup a snap.

LEMON-BUTTER TILAPIA WITH ALMONDS

Sometimes I want a nice meal without a ton of effort or wait time. Thankfully, I have this lemony, buttery fish that's super fast and totally tasty.
—Ramona Parris, Canton, GA

Takes: 10 min.
Makes: 4 servings

- 4 tilapia fillets (4 oz. each)
- ½ tsp. salt
- ¼ tsp. pepper
- 1 Tbsp. olive oil
- ¼ cup butter, cubed
- ¼ cup white wine or chicken broth
- 2 Tbsp. lemon juice
- ¼ cup sliced almonds

1. Sprinkle fillets with salt and pepper. In a large nonstick skillet, heat oil over medium heat. Add fillets; cook until fish just begins to flake easily with a fork, 2-3 minutes on each side. Remove and keep warm.

2. Add butter, wine and lemon juice to same pan; cook and stir until butter is melted. Serve with fish; sprinkle fish with almonds.

1 fillet with about 2 Tbsp. sauce and 2 Tbsp. almonds: 269 cal., 19g fat (8g sat. fat), 86mg chol., 427mg sod., 2g carb. (1g sugars, 1g fiber), 22g pro.

GARLIC HERBED
GRILLED TUNA STEAKS

GARLIC HERBED GRILLED TUNA STEAKS

After enjoying yellowfin tuna at a restaurant in southwest Florida, I came up with this recipe so I could enjoy the flavor of my favorite fish at my own home.

—Jan Huntington, Painesville, OH

Prep: 10 min. + marinating
Grill: 10 min. • **Makes:** 4 servings

- 2 Tbsp. lemon juice
- 1 Tbsp. olive oil
- 2 garlic cloves, minced
- 2 tsp. minced fresh thyme or ½ tsp. dried thyme
- 4 tuna steaks (6 oz. each)
- ¼ tsp. salt
- ¼ tsp. pepper

1. In a large container with a lid, combine the lemon juice, oil, garlic and thyme. Add tuna and turn to coat. Cover; refrigerate for up to 30 minutes, turning tuna over occasionally.
2. Remove tuna from bag; sprinkle with salt and pepper. Drain and discard marinade. Moisten a paper towel with cooking oil; using long-handled tongs, lightly coat the grill rack.
3. Grill tuna, covered, over medium-hot heat or broil 4 in. from the heat for 3-4 minutes on each side for medium-rare or until slightly pink in the center.

1 serving: 218 cal., 5g fat (1g sat. fat), 77mg chol., 211mg sod., 1g carb. (0 sugars, 0 fiber), 40g pro. **Diabetic exchanges:** 5 lean meat, ½ fat.

BAKED ITALIAN TILAPIA

BAKED ITALIAN TILAPIA

This dish is so simple, you might as well add it to your list of go-to recipes.

—Kimberly McGee, Mosheim, TN

Prep: 10 min. • **Bake:** 40 min.
Makes: 4 servings

- 4 tilapia fillets (6 oz. each)
- ¼ tsp. pepper
- 1 can (14½ oz.) diced tomatoes with basil, oregano and garlic, drained
- 1 large onion, halved and thinly sliced
- 1 medium green pepper, julienned
- ¼ cup shredded Parmesan cheese

1. Preheat oven to 350°. Place tilapia in a 13x9-in. baking dish coated with cooking spray; sprinkle with pepper. Spoon tomatoes over tilapia; top with onion and green pepper.
2. Cover and bake 30 minutes. Uncover; sprinkle with cheese. Bake until fish flakes easily with a fork, 10-15 minutes longer.

Freeze option: Cool fish mixture. Freeze in freezer containers. To use, partially thaw in refrigerator overnight. Heat through slowly in a covered skillet, stirring occasionally, until a thermometer inserted in fish reads 145°.

1 serving: 215 cal., 4g fat (2g sat. fat), 86mg chol., 645mg sod., 12g carb. (7g sugars, 2g fiber), 36g pro. **Diabetic exchanges:** 4 lean meat, 2 vegetable.

FIVE-SPICE TUNA

Adds Asian flair to tuna steaks with delightful results! If you want a bolder taste, marinate the tuna for 30 minutes.
—Linda Murray, Allenstown, NH

Takes: 30 min.
Makes: 4 servings

- 1 Tbsp. sugar
- 1 Tbsp. reduced-sodium soy sauce
- 1 Tbsp. sesame oil
- ½ tsp. Chinese five-spice powder
- ½ tsp. salt
- ¼ tsp. pepper
- 4 tuna steaks (1 in. thick and 6 oz. each)

1. In a large bowl of shallow dish, combine the first 6 ingredients. Add tuna steals and turn to coat. Refrigerate for 15 minutes.
2. Drain tuna steaks, discarding the marinade. Place tuna on a broiler pan coated with cooking spray. Broil 3-4 in. from the heat until fish flakes easily with a fork, 3-5 minutes on each side .

1 serving: 230 cal., 5g fat (1g sat. fat), 77mg chol., 509mg sod., 4g carb. (3g sugars, 0 fiber), 40g pro. **Diabetic exchanges:** 5 lean meat, ½ fat.

TOMATO-ARTICHOKE TILAPIA

My mom and I like tomatoes, capers and artichokes, so I use them together in this one-pan meal. The best part is that, on a busy night, I have all of the ingredients ready and waiting.
—Denise Klibert, Shreveport, LA

Takes: 15 min.
Makes: 4 servings

- 1 Tbsp. olive oil
- 1 can (14½ oz.) diced tomatoes with roasted garlic, drained
- 1 can (14 oz.) water-packed quartered artichoke hearts, drained
- 2 Tbsp. drained capers
- 4 tilapia fillets (6 oz. each)

1. In a large skillet, heat oil over medium heat. Add tomatoes, artichoke hearts and capers. Stirring occasionally cook until heated through, 3-5 minutes.
2. Arrange tilapia over tomato mixture. Cook, covered, until fish begins to flake easily with a fork, 6-8 minutes.

1 fillet with ¾ cup sauce: 246 cal., 5g fat (1g sat. fat), 83mg chol., 886mg sod., 15g carb. (6g sugars, 1g fiber), 35g pro.

Italian Fish Fillets: Substitute 1 medium julienned green pepper, 1 small julienned onion, ½ cup Italian salad dressing and ½ tsp. Italian seasoning for the first 4 ingredients. Cook 5 minutes or until vegetables are tender. Add 2 cans (14½ oz. each) diced tomatoes; bring to a boil. Add fish and cook as directed.

TOMATO-ARTICHOKE TILAPIA

CEDAR PLANK SCALLOPS

I got this idea from the fishmonger at our local farmers market and a kitchen store that had cedar cooking planks on sale. I made the first batch for my wife and me, made some adjustments and tried the recipe again with friends. Now all of my friends who tried them have gone out and bought cedar planks for cooking.

—Robert Halpert, Newburyport, MA

Prep: 10 min. + soaking
Grill: 15 min. • **Makes:** 4 servings

- 2 cedar grilling planks
- ¼ cup dry white wine
- 2 Tbsp. olive oil
- 2 tsp. minced fresh basil
- 1 tsp. minced fresh thyme
- 1 tsp. lime juice
- 12 sea scallops (about 1½ lbs.)

1. Soak planks in water at least 1 hour. In a large bowl, whisk wine, oil, basil, thyme and lime juice. Add scallops; gently toss to coat. Let stand 15 minutes.
2. Place planks on grill rack over direct medium heat. Cover and heat until light to medium smoke comes from the plank and the wood begins to crackle, 4-5 minutes. (This indicates the plank is ready.) Turn plank over and place on indirect heat. Drain scallops, discarding marinade. Place scallops on plank. Grill, covered, over indirect medium heat until firm and opaque, 10-12 minutes.

3 scallops: 142 cal., 3g fat (1g sat. fat), 41mg chol., 667mg sod., 6g carb. (0 sugars, 0 fiber), 21g pro. **Diabetic exchanges:** 3 lean meat, ½ starch, ½ fat.

HONEY-LIME RED SNAPPER

A two-ingredient marinade makes this a snap! If you can't find fresh snapper, substitute most any firm white fish. And if you can't find Key lime juice, use regular lime juice instead.
—Ken Hulme, Venice, FL

Prep: 5 min. + marinating
Broil: 15 min. • **Makes:** 4 servings

- ¾ cup Key lime juice
- ½ cup honey
- 4 red snapper fillets (6 oz. each)
- 2 tsp. chili powder

1. In a small bowl, combine lime juice and honey. Pour ½ cup into a container with a lid; add the fish and turn to coat. Refrigerate for up to 1 hour. Place remaining mixture in a small saucepan.
2. Drain the fish and discard marinade. Sprinkle fillets with chili powder; place on a greased broiler pan.
3. Broil 4-6 in. from the heat until fish flakes easily with a fork, 12-15 minutes.
4. Meanwhile, bring reserved lime juice mixture to a boil. Reduce the heat; simmer, uncovered, until reduced by half. Spoon over fillets.

1 serving: 277 cal., 2g fat (1g sat. fat), 60mg chol., 87mg sod., 31g carb. (29g sugars, 1g fiber), 34g pro. **Diabetic exchanges:** 5 lean meat, 2 starch.

STIR-FRIED SCALLOPS

Scallops meet mild tomato in this sublime stovetop supper. Try serving the saucy mixture over rice or angel hair pasta, and garnish the dish with cilantro if you'd like.

—Stephany Gocobachi, San Rafael, CA

Takes: 15 min.
Makes: 2 servings

- 1 small onion, chopped
- 3 garlic cloves, minced
- 1 Tbsp. olive oil
- ¾ lb. sea scallops, halved
- 2 medium plum tomatoes, chopped
- 2 Tbsp. lemon juice
- ⅛ tsp. pepper
- Hot cooked rice or pasta, optional

1. In a nonstick skillet or wok, stir-fry onion and garlic in hot oil until tender. Add scallops; stir-fry until scallops turn opaque. Add tomatoes; cook and stir until heated through, 1-2 minutes longer.
2. Stir in lemon juice and pepper. Serve with rice if desired.

1 cup: 213 cal., 8g fat (1g sat. fat), 41mg chol., 672mg sod., 14g carb. (4g sugars, 2g fiber), 22g pro.
Diabetic exchanges: 3 lean meat, 2 vegetable, 1½ fat.

STIR-FRIED SCALLOPS

SAGE-RUBBED SALMON

If you've always thought of sage with turkey, try it with salmon for a little taste of heaven. We serve this with rice, salad and sauteed green beans.

—Nicole Raskopf, Beacon, NY

Takes: 20 min.
Makes: 6 servings

- 2 Tbsp. minced fresh sage
- 1 tsp. garlic powder
- 1 tsp. kosher salt
- 1 tsp. freshly ground pepper
- 1 skin-on salmon fillet (1½ lbs.)
- 2 Tbsp. olive oil

1. Preheat oven to 375°. Mix the first 4 ingredients; rub onto flesh side of the salmon. Cut salmon into 6 portions.

2. In a large cast-iron skillet, heat oil over medium heat. Add the salmon, skin side down; cook 5 minutes. Transfer skillet to oven; bake just until the fish flakes easily with a fork, about 10 minutes.

3 oz. cooked fish: 220 cal., 15g fat (3g sat. fat), 57mg chol., 377mg sod., 1g carb. (0 sugars, 0 fiber), 19g pro. **Diabetic exchanges:** 3 lean meat.

CURRY SCALLOPS & RICE

Buttery scallops, colorful peppers and a fast rice mix tinged with curry...what's not to love about this stress-free main dish?

—*Taste of Home* Test Kitchen

Takes: 30 min.
Makes: 4 servings

- 1 pkg. (6¼ oz.) curry rice pilaf mix
- ¼ cup butter, divided
- 1½ lbs. sea scallops
- 1 pkg. (14 oz.) frozen pepper strips, thawed and chopped
- ¼ cup minced fresh parsley
- ¼ tsp. salt

1. Prepare pilaf mix according to package directions, using 1 Tbsp. butter.

2. Meanwhile, in a large skillet, saute scallops in the remaining 3 Tbsp. butter until firm and opaque. Remove and keep warm. In the same skillet, saute peppers until tender. Stir in the scallops, rice, parsley and salt.

1½ cups: 431 cal., 13g fat (7g sat. fat), 86mg chol., 998mg sod., 44g carb. (4g sugars, 3g fiber), 33g pro.

SAGE-RUBBED SALMON

PAN-SEARED COD

Cod has a soft, buttery appeal that goes great with cilantro, onions and crunchy pine nuts. This is the easiest, tastiest cod preparation I've found.

—Lucy Lu Wang, Seattle, WA

Takes: 25 min.
Makes: 2 servings

- 2 cod fillets (6 oz. each)
- ½ tsp. salt
- ¼ tsp. pepper
- 3 Tbsp. olive oil, divided
- ½ large sweet onion, thinly sliced
- ½ cup dry white wine
- ¼ cup coarsely chopped fresh cilantro
- 1 Tbsp. pine nuts or sliced almonds

1. Pat cod dry with paper towels; sprinkle with salt and pepper. In a large nonstick skillet, heat 2 Tbsp. oil over medium-high heat. Brown fillets lightly on both sides; remove from pan.
2. In same skillet, heat remaining 1 Tbsp. oil over medium heat. Add onion; cook and stir until softened, about 4-5 minutes. Stir in the wine; cook until onion is lightly browned, stirring occasionally, 3-4 minutes longer. Return cod to pan. Reduce heat to low; cook, covered, until fish just begins to flake easily with a fork, 2-3 minutes.
3. Remove cod from pan. Stir the cilantro and pine nuts into onion; serve with fish.

1 fillet with ¼ cup onion mixture: 378 cal., 24g fat (3g sat. fat), 65mg chol., 691mg sod., 8g carb. (5g sugars, 1g fiber), 28g pro.

★★★★★ **READER REVIEW**

"This turned out great! I doubled it so it made 4 servings. I also used cashews instead of pine nuts."

—TOMCATLOVER, TASTEOFHOME.COM

SPEEDY SHRIMP FLATBREADS

My husband and I are hooked on flatbread pizzas. I make at least one a week just to have something tasty around as a snack. This one came together easily because I had all the ingredients on hand.

—Cheryl Woodson, Liberty, MO

Takes: 15 min.
Makes: 2 servings

- 2 naan flatbreads or whole pita breads
- 1 pkg. (5.2 oz.) garlic-herb spreadable cheese
- ½ lb. peeled and deveined cooked shrimp (31-40 per lb.)
- ½ cup chopped oil-packed sun-dried tomatoes
- ¼ cup fresh basil leaves
- Lemon wedges, optional

Preheat oven to 400°. Place flatbreads on a baking sheet. Spread with cheese; top with shrimp and tomatoes. Bake until heated through, 4-6 minutes. Sprinkle with basil. If desired, serve with lemon wedges.

1 flatbread: 634 cal., 41g fat (24g sat. fat), 263mg chol., 1163mg sod., 38g carb. (3g sugars, 3g fiber), 33g pro.

SPEEDY SHRIMP FLATBREADS

POTATO-CRUSTED SNAPPER

You'll reel in raves with this seafood supper. The crispy potato-crusted fillets are great with steamed green beans and rice pilaf.

—Athena Russell, Greenville, SC

Takes: 30 min.
Makes: 4 servings

- 2 large eggs, beaten
- 1½ cups mashed potato flakes
- 2 tsp. dried thyme
- 4 red snapper fillets (6 oz. each)
- ½ tsp. salt
- ¼ tsp. pepper
- ¼ cup olive oil

1. Place the eggs in a shallow bowl. In another shallow bowl, combine potato flakes and thyme. Sprinkle fillets with salt and pepper. Dip in eggs and coat with potato mixture.
2. In a large skillet, cook fillets in oil in batches over medium heat until the fish flakes easily with a fork, 4-5 minutes on each side.

1 serving: 368 cal., 17g fat (3g sat. fat), 126mg chol., 424mg sod., 14g carb. (0 sugars, 1g fiber), 37g pro.

PRESSURE-COOKER DILL PENNE WITH SMOKED SALMON

I love making one-pot pastas in my pressure cooker. Every noodle soaks up the flavors of the delicious ingredients you throw in. I tried this version with some leftover smoked fish and fresh dill, and boom—this was born. It's now a staple in our house because it's on the table in half an hour and the kids love it!

—Shannon Dobos, Calgary, AB

Takes: 20 min.
Makes: 6 servings

- 2¼ cups chicken broth
- ½ lb. smoked salmon fillets, flaked
- ½ cup heavy whipping cream
- 2 Tbsp. snipped fresh dill
- ½ tsp. pepper
- 12 oz. uncooked penne pasta
- Optional: Additional dill and lemon slices

Place broth, salmon, cream, dill and pepper in a 6-qt. electric pressure cooker; top with penne (do not stir). Lock lid; close the pressure-release valve. Adjust to pressure-cook on high for 8 minutes. Quick-release pressure. Gently stir before serving. If desired, top with additional dill and lemon slices.

1¼ cups: 322 cal., 10g fat (5g sat. fat), 33mg chol., 672mg sod., 42g carb. (3g sugars, 2g fiber), 15g pro.

DAD'S FAMOUS STUFFIES

DAD'S FAMOUS STUFFIES

The third of July is almost as important as the Fourth in my family. We make these stuffies on the third every year, and it's an event in and of itself!

—Karen Barros, Bristol, RI

Prep: 1¼ hours • **Bake:** 20 min.
Makes: 10 servings

- 20 fresh large quahog clams (about 10 lbs.)
- 1 lb. hot chourico or linguica (smoked Portuguese sausage) or fully cooked Spanish chorizo
- 1 large onion, chopped (about 2 cups)
- 3 tsp. seafood seasoning
- 1 pkg. (14 oz.) herb stuffing cubes
- 1 cup water
- Optional: Lemon wedges and hot pepper sauce

1. Add 2 in. water to a stockpot. Add the clams and chourico; bring to a boil. Cover and steam until the clams open, 15-20 minutes.
2. Remove the clams and sausage from pot, reserving 2 cups cooking liquid; cool slightly. Discard any of the unopened clams.
3. Preheat oven to 350°. Remove clam meat from shells. Separate shells; reserve 30 half-shells for stuffing. Place clam meat in a food processor; process until finely chopped. Transfer to a large bowl.
4. Remove casings from sausage; cut sausage into 1½-in. pieces. Place in a food processor; process until finely chopped. Add sausage, onion and seafood seasoning to chopped clams. Stir in stuffing cubes. Add reserved cooking liquid and enough water to reach desired moistness, about 1 cup.
5. Spoon the clam mixture into the reserved shells. Place in 15x10x1-in. baking pans. Bake until heated through, 15-20 minutes. Preheat broiler.
6. Broil the clams 4-6 in. from the heat until golden brown, 4-5 minutes . If desired, serve with lemon wedges and the pepper sauce.

Freeze option: Cover and freeze unbaked stuffed clams in a 15x10x1-in. baking pan until firm. Transfer to freezer containers; return to freezer. To use, place 3 stuffed clams on a microwave-safe plate. Cover with a paper towel; microwave on high until heated through, 3-4 minutes. Serve as directed.

3 stuffed clams: 296 cal., 11g fat (3g sat. fat), 71mg chol., 1188mg sod., 34g carb. (3g sugars, 2g fiber), 18g pro.

ARTICHOKE COD WITH SUN-DRIED TOMATOES

ARTICHOKE COD WITH SUN-DRIED TOMATOES

I like to serve this over a bed of greens, pasta or quinoa. A squeeze of lemon gives it another layer of freshness.
—Hiroko Miles, El Dorado Hills, CA

Takes: 30 min.
Makes: 6 servings

- 1 can (14 oz.) quartered water-packed artichoke hearts, drained
- ½ cup julienned soft sun-dried tomatoes (not packed in oil)
- 2 green onions, chopped
- 3 Tbsp. olive oil
- 1 garlic clove, minced
- 6 cod fillets (6 oz. each)
- 1 tsp. salt
- ½ tsp. pepper
- Optional: Salad greens and lemon wedges

1. Preheat oven to 400°. In a small bowl, combine the first 5 ingredients; toss to combine.
2. Sprinkle both sides of cod with salt and pepper; place in a 13x9-in. baking dish coated with cooking spray. Top with the artichoke mixture.
3. Bake, uncovered, until fish just begins to flake easily with a fork, 15-20 minutes. If desired, serve over greens with lemon wedges.

1 fillet with ⅓ cup artichoke mixture: 231 cal., 8g fat (1g sat. fat), 65mg chol., 665mg sod., 9g carb. (3g sugars, 2g fiber), 29g pro.

OVEN-ROASTED SALMON

OVEN-ROASTED SALMON

When I'm starving after work, I want a fast meal with a no-fail technique. Roasted salmon is super tender and has a delicate sweetness. It's also an easy wowza for company.
—Jeanne Ambrose, Milwaukee, WI

Takes: 20 min.
Makes: 4 servings

- 1 center-cut salmon fillet (1½ lbs.)
- 1 Tbsp. olive oil
- ½ tsp. salt
- ¼ tsp. pepper

1. Place a large cast-iron or other ovenproof skillet in a cold oven. Preheat oven to 450°. Meanwhile, brush the salmon with oil and sprinkle with salt and pepper.
2. Carefully remove skillet from oven. Place fish, skin side down, in skillet. Return to oven; bake uncovered, until salmon flakes easily and a thermometer reads 125°, 14-18 minutes. Cut salmon into 4 equal portions.

1 fillet: 295 cal., 19g fat (4g sat. fat), 85mg chol., 380mg sod., 0 carb. (0 sugars, 0 fiber), 29g pro. **Diabetic exchanges:** 4 lean meat, ½ fat.

MEATLESS ENTREES

FETA-STUFFED PORTOBELLO MUSHROOMS
P. 186

1

2

3

4

5

MEATLESS DOESN'T HAVE TO MEAN BLAND AND BORING. SEE HOW EASY IT IS TO IMPRESS YOUR GANG WITH THESE 5-INGREDIENT FAVORITES.

THREE-VEGETABLE
PASTA SAUCE

PIZZA CAPRESE

One of my favorite pizzas is so simple to make and comes together so quickly. Pizza caprese is simply heirloom tomatoes, fresh mozzarella and really good extra virgin olive oil. I could have this tasty pie every day!

—Beth Berlin, Oak Creek, WI

Takes: 30 min.
Makes: 6 servings

- 1 pkg. (6½ oz.) pizza crust mix
- 2 Tbsp. extra virgin olive oil, divided
- 2 garlic cloves, thinly sliced
- 1 large tomato, thinly sliced
- 4 oz. fresh mozzarella cheese, sliced
- ⅓ cup loosely packed basil leaves

1. Preheat oven to 425°. Prepare the pizza dough according to package directions. With floured hands, press dough onto a greased 12-in. pizza pan.

2. Drizzle 1 Tbsp. olive oil over dough and sprinkle with sliced garlic. Bake until crust is lightly browned, 10-12 minutes. Top with the tomato and fresh mozzarella; bake until cheese is melted, 5-7 minutes longer. Drizzle with remaining 1 Tbsp. olive oil and top with basil. Serve pizza immediately.

1 piece: 208 cal., 9g fat (3g sat. fat), 15mg chol., 196mg sod., 23g carb. (3g sugars, 1g fiber), 7g pro.

THREE-VEGETABLE PASTA SAUCE

In an effort to sneak vegetables into my family's food, I created this zesty meat-free sauce of cauliflowerets, baby spinach and tomatoes.

—Chase Miller, Gatesville, TX

Prep: 20 min. • **Cook:** 2 hours
Makes: 3 cups

- 2 cups fresh cauliflowerets
- 2 cans (14½ oz. each) diced tomatoes, undrained
- 4 cups fresh baby spinach (about 4 oz.)
- ½ tsp. salt
- ½ tsp. garlic powder
- Hot cooked pasta

1. In a large saucepan, place a steamer basket over 1 in. of water. Place cauliflowerets in basket. Bring the water to a boil. Reduce the heat to maintain a simmer; steam, covered, about 10-12 minutes or until tender. Cool slightly.

2. Place cauliflower in a food processor; process until pureed. Transfer to a large saucepan; stir in the tomatoes, spinach, salt and garlic powder. Bring to a boil. Reduce the heat; simmer, uncovered, about 2 hours or until flavors are blended, stirring occasionally. Serve with pasta.

¾ cup: 61 cal., 0 fat (0 sat. fat), 0 chol., 595mg sod., 14g carb. (8g sugars, 5g fiber), 4g pro.

PIZZA CAPRESE

MARINARA SAUCE

My mother, who was Italian American, called marinara sauce "gravy." She made this sauce in big batches several times a month, so it was a staple on our dinner table. A mouthwatering aroma filled the house each time she cooked it.

—James Grimes, Frenchtown, NJ

Prep: 20 min. • **Cook:** 1 hour
Makes: 5 cups

- 2 cans (28 oz. each) whole tomatoes
- 1 large onion, finely chopped
- 4 garlic cloves, minced
- 3 Tbsp. extra virgin olive oil
- ¼ cup chopped fresh basil
- 1½ tsp. dried oregano
- ¾ tsp. salt
- ¼ tsp. pepper

In a large saucepan, heat oil over medium-high heat. Add the onions; cook and stir until tender, 3-5 minutes. Add garlic; cook and stir 1 minute longer. Stir in remaining ingredients. Bring to a boil. Reduce heat; cover and simmer until thickened and the flavors are blended, 30-45 minutes, stirring occasionally and breaking up tomatoes with wooden spoon.

½ cup: 44 cal., 4g fat (1g sat. fat), 0 chol., 178mg sod., 2g carb. (1g sugars, 0 fiber), 0 pro.

BEAN & CHEESE QUESADILLAS

My son doesn't eat meat, so I created this recipe as a way for me to cook one meal for the family instead of two. It's so easy that my toddler grandson helps me make it!
—Tina McMullen, Salina, KS

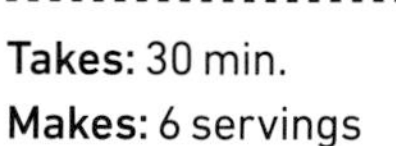

Takes: 30 min.
Makes: 6 servings

- 1 can (16 oz.) refried beans
- ½ cup canned petite diced tomatoes
- 2 green onions, chopped
- 12 flour tortillas (8 in.)
- 2 cups shredded cheddar cheese
- Optional: Sour cream and salsa

1. In a small bowl, mix beans, tomatoes and green onions. Spread half the tortillas with bean mixture. Sprinkle with cheddar cheese; top with the remaining tortillas.

2. Heat a griddle over medium heat. Place tortillas on griddle in batches. Cook until golden brown and cheese is melted, 2-3 minutes on each side. If desired, serve with sour cream and salsa.

1 quesadilla: 544 cal., 21g fat (9g sat. fat), 37mg chol., 1028mg sod., 67g carb. (1g sugars, 6g fiber), 21g pro.

Bacon-Tomato Quesadillas: Use 10 medium tomatoes, seeded and finely chopped; 8 bacon strips, cooked and crumbled; and 3 cups (12 oz.) shredded Mexican cheese blend for the first 3 ingredients. Omit cheddar cheese. Assemble and cook as directed.

BEAN & CHEESE QUESADILLAS

AIR-FRYER SPINACH FETA TURNOVERS

These quick and easy turnovers are one of my wife's favorite entrees. The refrigerated pizza dough makes preparation a snap!
—David Baruch, Weston, FL

Takes: 30 min. **Makes:** 4 servings

- 2 large eggs
- 1 pkg. (10 oz.) frozen spinach, thawed, squeezed dry and chopped
- ¾ cup crumbled feta cheese
- 2 garlic cloves, minced
- ¼ tsp. pepper
- 1 tube (13.8 oz.) refrigerated pizza crust
- Refrigerated tzatziki sauce, optional

1. Preheat air fryer to 425°. In a bowl, whisk eggs; set aside 1 Tbsp. of eggs. Combine the spinach, feta cheese, garlic, pepper and the remaining beaten eggs.

2. Unroll pizza crust; roll into a 12-in. square. Cut into four 6-in. squares. Top each square with about ⅓ cup spinach mixture. Fold into a triangle and pinch edges to seal. Cut slits in top; brush with reserved egg.

3. In batches if necessary, place the triangles in a single layer on a greased tray in air-fryer basket. Cook until golden brown, 10-12 minutes. If desired, serve with tzatziki sauce.

1 turnover: 361 cal., 9g fat (4g sat. fat), 104mg chol., 936mg sod., 51g carb. (7g sugars, 4g fiber), 17g pro.

AIR-FRYER SPINACH FETA TURNOVERS

LAZY LASAGNA FOR 2

Lasagna may seem as if it's a lot of work on a busy evening, but one day, when I had a craving for it, I devised this simple recipe and it worked out beautifully.

—Carol Mead, Los Alamos, NM

Takes: 30 min.
Makes: 2 servings

- 1 cup meatless pasta sauce
- ¾ cup shredded part-skim mozzarella cheese
- ½ cup 4% cottage cheese
- 1½ cups cooked wide egg noodles
- 2 Tbsp. grated Parmesan cheese
- Chopped fresh parsley, optional

1. Warm the pasta sauce; stir in mozzarella and cottage cheeses. Fold in egg noodles. Pour into 2 greased 2-cup baking dishes. Sprinkle with Parmesan cheese.
2. Bake, uncovered, at 375° until bubbly, about 20 minutes. If desired, top with parsley.
1 lasagna: 399 cal., 16g fat (8g sat. fat), 68mg chol., 1120mg sod., 37g carb. (12g sugars, 3g fiber), 25g pro.

LAZY LASAGNA FOR 2

GARLIC SPAGHETTI

GARLIC SPAGHETTI

I make this family favorite at least two or three times a month. It's wonderful with a salad and fresh Italian bread. Besides being easy to prepare, this meatless main dish is easy on the pocketbook at just a few cents per serving.

—Jackie Messina, Chardon, OH

Takes: 30 min.
Makes: 6 servings

- 1 pkg. (16 oz.) spaghetti
- 10 garlic cloves, minced
- ¼ cup olive oil
- ¼ cup minced fresh parsley
- 2 tsp. dried oregano or 2 Tbsp. minced fresh oregano
- 1 tsp. salt
- ¼ tsp. pepper
- ½ cup grated Parmesan cheese

Cook spaghetti according to package directions. Meanwhile, in a skillet over low heat, cook garlic in oil until lightly browned. Remove from the heat; stir in the parsley, oregano, salt and pepper. Drain the spaghetti; place in a large bowl. Add garlic mixture and Parmesan cheese; toss to coat.

1⅓ cups: 398 cal., 12g fat (2g sat. fat), 6mg chol., 521mg sod., 59g carb. (2g sugars, 3g fiber), 12g pro.

AVOCADO QUESADILLAS

AVOCADO QUESADILLAS

Avocado slices give quesadillas a nutritional boost. Even my picky son likes them! Add a little cooked chicken or beef for extra protein.

—Debbie Limas, North Andover, MA

Takes: 20 min.
Makes: 4 servings

- 1 Tbsp. canola oil
- 16 corn tortillas (6 in.)
- 2 cups shredded Mexican cheese blend
- 1 cup pico de gallo
- 1 large ripe avocado, peeled and thinly sliced
- 3 Tbsp. minced fresh cilantro
- Additional pico de gallo

1. Grease a griddle with oil; heat over medium heat. Lightly sprinkle tortillas with water to moisten.

2. Place 8 tortillas on griddle; sprinkle with cheese. After the cheese has melted slightly, top with 1 cup pico de gallo, avocado and cilantro. Top with remaining tortillas.

3. Cook until tortillas are lightly browned and cheese is melted, 3-4 minutes on each side. Serve with additional pico de gallo.

2 quesadillas: 611 cal., 37g fat (15g sat. fat), 50mg chol., 455mg sod., 54g carb. (2g sugars, 12g fiber), 20g pro.

ROASTED CURRIED CHICKPEAS & CAULIFLOWER

When you don't have much time to cook, try roasting potatoes and cauliflower with chickpeas for a warm-you-up dinner. Add chicken or tofu to the sheet pan if you like.

—Pam Correll, Brockport, PA

Prep: 15 min. • **Bake:** 30 min.
Makes: 4 servings

- 2 lbs. potatoes (about 4 medium), peeled and cut into ½-in. cubes
- 1 small head cauliflower, broken into florets (about 3 cups)
- 1 can (15 oz.) chickpeas or garbanzo beans, rinsed and drained
- 3 Tbsp. olive oil
- 2 tsp. curry powder
- ¾ tsp. salt
- ¼ tsp. pepper
- 3 Tbsp. minced fresh cilantro or parsley

1. Preheat oven to 400°. Place first 7 ingredients in a large bowl; toss to coat. Transfer to a 15x10x1-in. baking pan coated with cooking spray.
2. Roast until vegetables are tender, 30-35 minutes, stirring occasionally. Sprinkle with fresh cilantro.

1½ cups: 339 cal., 13g fat (2g sat. fat), 0 chol., 605mg sod., 51g carb. (6g sugars, 8g fiber), 8g pro. **Diabetic exchanges:** 3 starch, 2 fat, 1 vegetable, 1 lean meat.

MAKEOVER MACARONI & CHEESE

This is one of my family's favorites. Creamy and cheesy, this lightened-up classic will become a must-have at your house, too!

—Nancy Langrock, Southbury, CT

Takes: 30 min.
Makes: 8 servings

- 1 pkg. (16 oz.) elbow macaroni
- 2 Tbsp. all-purpose flour
- 2 cups fat-free milk
- 1 pkg. (16 oz.) reduced-fat Velveeta, cubed
- 1 cup shredded sharp cheddar cheese, divided

1. Cook macaroni according to package directions. Meanwhile, in a large saucepan, combine flour and milk until smooth. Bring to a boil; cook and stir for 2 minutes or until thickened. Stir in Velveeta and ½ cup cheddar cheese until smooth. Drain macaroni; stir into the cheese sauce.

2. Remove from heat; sprinkle with remaining cheese. Cover and let stand for 5 minutes or until cheese is melted.

1 cup: 403 cal., 11g fat (6g sat. fat), 36mg chol., 944mg sod., 54g carb. (9g sugars, 2g fiber), 23g pro.

KITCHEN-SINK SOFT TACOS

My kids invented this recipe by throwing some taco spice on leftover sloppy joes. I have to admit, they are delicious. Though they're excellent after school, we also love them as a tasty yet timely weekend lunch.

—Darlene King, Regina, SK

Takes: 15 min.
Makes: 6 servings

- ½ cup uncooked instant rice
- 1 can (15 oz.) chili with beans
- 1 tsp. taco seasoning
- 12 flour tortillas (6 in.), warmed
- 1 cup shredded cheddar cheese

1. Cook the rice according to package directions. In a microwave-safe bowl, combine the chili and taco seasoning. Cover and microwave on high for 2-3 minutes or until the mixture is heated through.

2. Spoon rice and chili onto tortillas; sprinkle with cheese. Fold sides of tortillas over filling.

2 each: 347 cal., 13g fat (5g sat. fat), 27mg chol., 941mg sod., 43g carb. (1g sugars, 3g fiber), 15g pro.

PASTA WITH ROASTED GARLIC & TOMATOES

GREEK SPINACH BAKE

Spanakopita is the Greek name for this traditional dish featuring spinach and feta cheese. You can serve it as a meatless main dish or even a change-of-pace side.

—Sharon Olney, Galt, CA

Prep: 10 min. • **Bake:** 1 hour
Makes: 6 servings

- 2 cups 4% cottage cheese
- 1 pkg. (10 oz.) frozen chopped spinach, thawed and squeezed dry
- 8 oz. crumbled feta cheese
- 6 Tbsp. all-purpose flour
- ½ tsp. pepper
- ¼ tsp. salt
- 4 large eggs, lightly beaten

1. Preheat oven to 350°. In a large bowl, combine the cottage cheese, spinach and feta cheese. Stir in the flour, pepper and salt. Add eggs and mix well.
2. Spoon into a greased 9-in. square baking dish. Bake, uncovered, until a thermometer reads 160°, about 1 hour.

1 serving: 262 cal., 13g fat (7g sat. fat), 178mg chol., 838mg sod., 14g carb. (4g sugars, 3g fiber), 21g pro.

PASTA WITH ROASTED GARLIC & TOMATOES

Here's a simple sauce with just four ingredients, and it's savory enough for a fancy party. I use bow tie pasta, but penne pasta works, too.

—Aysha Schurman, Ammon, ID

Takes: 20 min.
Makes: 4 servings

- 1½ lbs. cherry tomatoes
- 12 garlic cloves, peeled
- 3 Tbsp. olive oil
- 3 cups uncooked bow tie pasta
- 4 oz. (½ cup) cream cheese, softened
- ½ tsp. salt

1. Preheat oven to 450°. In a bowl, toss tomatoes and garlic cloves with oil; transfer to a greased 15x10x1-in. baking pan. Roast 14-16 minutes or until very soft. Meanwhile, cook pasta according to package directions.
2. Cool tomato mixture slightly. Reserve 12 tomatoes for serving with pasta. Transfer remaining tomato mixture to a food processor. Add cream cheese and salt; process until smooth. Transfer to a large bowl.
3. Drain pasta; add to tomato mixture and toss to coat. Top with reserved tomatoes.

1 cup: 441 cal., 22g fat (8g sat. fat), 32mg chol., 401mg sod., 52g carb. (7g sugars, 4g fiber), 12g pro.

GREEK SPINACH BAKE

SAGE & BROWNED BUTTER RAVIOLI

After enjoying a similar dish in Italy, we came home and planted sage so could recreate it. It is a such a quick and easy weeknight supper using the fruits of our labor, and brings back fond memories of our trip.
—Rhonda Hamilton, Portsmouth, OH

Takes: 30 min.
Makes: 4 servings

- 1 pkg. (20 oz.) refrigerated cheese ravioli or 2 pkg. (9 oz. each) mushroom agnolotti
- ½ cup butter, cubed
- ½ cup coarsely chopped fresh sage
- ½ tsp. salt
- 2 Tbsp. lemon juice
- ¼ cup shredded Parmesan cheese

1. Cook ravioli according to package directions. In a large heavy saucepan, melt butter over medium heat. Heat 5-7 minutes or until golden brown, stirring constantly. Immediately stir in sage and salt; remove from heat.
2. Drain ravioli, reserving 2 Tbsp. pasta water. Add ravioli, pasta water and lemon juice to butter mixture; gently toss to coat. Serve with the cheese.

1 cup: 621 cal., 34g fat (21g sat. fat), 120mg chol., 1103mg sod., 58g carb. (2g sugars, 3g fiber), 23g pro.

SAGE & BROWNED BUTTER RAVIOLI

TOMATO ALFREDO PASTA

Unable to decide between topping pasta with tomato or Alfredo sauce, I combined them into one.
—Darlene Brenden, Salem, OR

Takes: 20 min.
Makes: 4 servings

- 8 oz. uncooked ziti or small tube pasta
- 1 can (14½ oz.) Italian stewed tomatoes, undrained
- ½ cup heavy whipping cream
- ¼ cup chopped fresh basil or 1½ tsp. dried basil
- ½ cup grated Parmesan cheese

1. Cook pasta according to package directions. Meanwhile, in a large skillet, bring the tomatoes to a boil. Cook until most of the liquid is evaporated, about 5 minutes. Reduce heat.
2. Stir in the cream and basil; heat through (do not boil). Drain pasta. Add pasta and Parmesan cheese to sauce; toss to coat.
1 cup: 380 cal., 15g fat (9g sat. fat), 49mg chol., 543mg sod., 50g carb. (8g sugars, 4g fiber), 13g pro.

HOMEMADE PASTA

Try your hand at homemade pasta with this easy spinach dough. You will not need a pasta maker or any other special equipment!
—*Taste of Home* Test Kitchen

Prep: 30 min. + standing
Cook: 10 min./batch
Makes: 8 servings

- 1 pkg. (10 oz.) frozen chopped spinach, thawed and squeezed dry
- ¼ cup packed fresh parsley sprigs
- 3½ to 4 cups all-purpose flour
- ½ tsp. salt
- 4 large eggs
- 3 Tbsp. water
- 1 Tbsp. olive oil
- Marinara sauce

1. Place spinach and fresh parsley in a food processor; cover and process until finely chopped. Add 3½ cups flour and salt; process until blended. Add the eggs, water and oil. Process until dough forms a ball, 15-20 seconds.
2. Turn onto a floured surface; knead until smooth and elastic, 8-10 minutes, adding remaining flour if necessary. Cover and let rest for 30 minutes. Divide the dough into fourths.
3. On a floured surface, roll each portion to 1/16-in. thickness. Dust top of dough with flour to prevent sticking; cut into ¼-in. slices. Separate the slices; allow the noodles to dry on clean kitchen towels for at least 1 hour before cooking.
4. To cook, fill a Dutch oven three-fourths full with water. Bring to a boil. Add noodles in batches; cook, uncovered, until tender, 8-10 minutes. Drain. Serve with sauce.

1 cup: 259 cal., 5g fat (1g sat. fat), 106mg chol., 211mg sod., 43g carb. (1g sugars, 3g fiber), 10g pro.

POLENTA LASAGNA

POLENTA LASAGNA

Using polenta instead of pasta gives you an amazing twist on traditional lasagna. We love the easy assembly.

—Yevgeniya Farrer, Fremont, CA

Takes: 25 min.
Makes: 4 servings

- 1½ cups marinara sauce
- 1 tsp. garlic powder
- 1 tsp. herbes de Provence
- 1 tube (18 oz.) polenta, cut into 10 slices
- 1½ cups shredded part-skim mozzarella cheese

1. In a small bowl, mix marinara sauce, garlic powder and herbes de Provence. Arrange half the polenta slices in a greased 8-in. skillet. Top with half the sauce; sprinkle with ¾ cup cheese. Repeat layers.
2. Cook, uncovered, over medium heat 12-14 minutes or until bubbly. Cover; cook 2-3 minutes longer or until cheese is melted.

1 piece: 280 cal., 10g fat (5g sat. fat), 25mg chol., 1120mg sod., 32g carb. (8g sugars, 3g fiber), 14g pro.

FETA-STUFFED PORTOBELLO MUSHROOMS

My husband just adores mushrooms, and portobello mushrooms have loads of room for stuffing with feta cheese and pesto.

—Amy Martell, Canton, PA

Takes: 20 min.
Makes: 4 servings

- 4 large portobello mushrooms (4 to 4½ in. each)
- 2 Tbsp. olive oil
- 1 garlic clove, minced
- ¼ tsp. salt
- 1 cup (4 oz.) crumbled feta cheese
- ½ cup prepared pesto

1. Remove and discard stems from mushrooms; with a spoon, scrape and remove gills. In a small bowl, combine oil and garlic; brush over mushrooms. Sprinkle with salt. In a small bowl, combine cheese and pesto.
2. Place mushrooms on a piece of greased heavy-duty foil (about 12-in. square). Grill mushrooms, stem side up, covered, over medium heat or broil 4 in. from heat 8-10 minutes, until mushrooms are tender. Spoon cheese mixture into mushrooms; grill, covered, 2-3 minutes or until filling is heated through.

1 stuffed mushroom: 273 cal., 22g fat (5g sat. fat), 15mg chol., 783mg sod., 9g carb. (3g sugars, 3g fiber), 9g pro.

FETA-STUFFED PORTOBELLO MUSHROOMS

CHEESY SUMMER SQUASH FLATBREADS

CHEESY SUMMER SQUASH FLATBREADS

When you want a meatless meal with Mediterranean style, these flatbreads smothered with squash, hummus and mozzarella deliver the goods.
—Matthew Hass, Ellison Bay, WI

Takes: 30 min.
Makes: 4 servings

- 3 small yellow summer squash, sliced ¼ in. thick
- 1 Tbsp. olive oil
- ½ tsp. salt
- 2 cups fresh baby spinach, coarsely chopped
- 2 naan flatbreads
- ⅓ cup roasted red pepper hummus
- 1 carton (8 oz.) fresh mozzarella cheese pearls
- Pepper

1. Preheat oven to 425°. Toss summer squash with oil and salt; spread evenly in a 15x10x1-in. baking pan. Roast squash until tender, 8-10 minutes. Transfer to a bowl; stir in the fresh baby spinach.

2. Place naan on a baking sheet; spread with the hummus. Top with the squash mixture and cheese. Bake on a lower oven rack just until the cheese is melted, 4-6 minutes. Sprinkle with pepper.

½ topped flatbread: 332 cal., 20g fat (9g sat. fat), 47mg chol., 737mg sod., 24g carb. (7g sugars, 3g fiber), 15g pro.

HOMEMADE MARINARA SAUCE

This quick and easy homemade marinara sauce is my kids' favorite. It works fantastic with spaghetti, and my kids love it in meatball subs, too.
—Cara Bjornlie, Detroit Lakes, MN

Takes: 30 min. • **Makes:** 7 cups

- 1 Tbsp. olive oil
- 1 small onion, chopped
- 2 garlic cloves, minced
- 2 cans (28 oz. each) Italian crushed tomatoes
- 1 Tbsp. Italian seasoning
- 1 to 2 Tbsp. sugar
- ½ tsp. salt
- ½ tsp. pepper

In a large saucepan, heat the oil over medium heat. Add the onion; cook and stir until softened, 3-4 minutes. Add the garlic; cook 1 minute longer. Add tomatoes, Italian seasoning, sugar, salt and pepper; bring to a boil. Reduce heat; simmer, covered, 10 minutes.

About ¾ cup: 91 cal., 2g fat (0 sat. fat), 0 chol., 489mg sod., 12g carb. (8g sugars, 3g fiber), 3g pro. **Diabetic exchanges:** 2 vegetable, ½ fat.

HOMEMADE MARINARA SAUCE

STUFFED PASTA SHELLS

STUFFED PASTA SHELLS

These savory shells never fail to make a big impression, even though the recipe is very easy. One or two of these shells makes a fantastic individual serving at a potluck, so a single batch goes a long way.

—Jena Coffey, St. Louis, MO

Prep: 15 min. • **Bake:** 30 min.
Makes: 12 servings

- 4 cups shredded mozzarella cheese
- 1 carton (15 oz.) ricotta cheese
- 1 pkg. (10 oz.) frozen chopped spinach, thawed and squeezed dry
- 1 pkg. (12 oz.) jumbo pasta shells, cooked and drained
- 3½ cups spaghetti sauce
- Grated Parmesan cheese, optional

Preheat oven to 350°. Combine cheeses and spinach; stuff into shells. Arrange in a greased 13x9-in. baking dish. Pour spaghetti sauce over the shells. Cover and bake until heated through, about 30 minutes. If desired, sprinkle with Parmesan after baking.

1 serving: 314 cal., 13g fat (7g sat. fat), 44mg chol., 576mg sod., 32g carb. (9g sugars, 3g fiber), 18g pro.

CHEESE RAVIOLI WITH VEGGIES

CHEESE RAVIOLI WITH VEGGIES

When pasta and veggies are on the menu, my sons get to the table fast. The frozen medley is so convenient, but sometimes I throw in peas, corn, broccoli or zucchini instead.

—Amy Burns, Charleston, IL

Takes: 25 min.
Makes: 6 servings

- 1 pkg. (25 oz.) frozen cheese ravioli
- 1 pkg. (16 oz.) frozen California-blend vegetables
- ¼ cup butter, melted
- ¼ tsp. salt-free seasoning blend
- ¼ cup shredded Parmesan cheese

1. Fill a 6-qt. stockpot two-thirds full with water; bring to a boil. Add frozen ravioli and vegetable blend; return to a boil. Cook 6-8 minutes or until ravioli and vegetables are tender; drain.
2. Gently stir in the butter. Sprinkle with seasoning blend and cheese.

1 cup: 339 cal., 15g fat (9g sat. fat), 73mg chol., 391mg sod., 35g carb. (2g sugars, 3g fiber), 15g pro.

SOUPS & SANDWICHES

HAWAIIAN PULLED PORK LETTUCE WRAPS
P. 203

1

2

3

4

5

MEALTIME IS A SNAP WHEN YOU SERVE UP THE CLASSIC PAIRING OF SOUP AND SANDWICH—WITH ONLY A HANDFUL OF INGREDIENTS.

GRILLED PIMIENTO CHEESE SANDWICHES

GRILLED PIMIENTO CHEESE SANDWICHES

Rich and creamy pimiento cheese is a southern favorite. It makes a tasty grilled cheese sandwich, especially with sweet hot pepper jelly. Serve this with a crisp salad for a fantastic lunch.

—Amy Freeze, Avon Park, FL

Takes: 20 min.
Makes: 2 servings

- 4 slices sourdough bread
- ¼ cup butter, softened
- ½ cup refrigerated pimiento cheese
- 2 Tbsp. pepper jelly
- 6 cooked thick-sliced bacon strips

1. Spread both sides of bread slices with butter. In a large skillet, toast bread on 1 side over medium heat until golden brown, 3-4 minutes.

2. Remove from heat; place toasted side up. Spread cheese over toasted bread slices. Top 2 slices with jelly, then with bacon. Top with remaining bread slices, cheese facing inward. Cook until the bread is golden brown and cheese is melted, 3-4 minutes on each side. If desired, serve with additional jelly.

1 sandwich: 869 cal., 52g fat (28g sat. fat), 105mg chol., 1856mg sod., 70g carb. (19g sugars, 2g fiber), 27g pro.

OLD-FASHIONED TOMATO SOUP

OLD-FASHIONED TOMATO SOUP

My mother made this soup when I was a child, and it was always a favorite. After 75 years, it still is! Her cellar was filled with home-canned vegetables, so the soup's basic ingredient was right at hand. It never took her long to make a kettle of this wonderful soup.

—Wilma Miller, Port Angeles, WA

Takes: 20 min.
Makes: 6 servings (1½ qt.)

- 1 can (14½ oz.) diced tomatoes, undrained
- ½ tsp. baking soda
- ¼ to ½ tsp. garlic salt
- ⅛ tsp. pepper
- Salt to taste, optional
- 1 qt. milk
- 2 Tbsp. butter
- Minced fresh parsley, optional

In a large saucepan, bring tomatoes to a boil. Add baking soda, garlic salt, pepper and, if desired, salt. Reduce heat; add milk and butter. Heat through but do not boil. Garnish with parsley if desired.

1 cup: 148 cal., 9g fat (6g sat. fat), 32mg chol., 423mg sod., 10g carb. (9g sugars, 1g fiber), 6g pro.

TEST KITCHEN TIP
You can replace the canned tomatoes with 2 cups of home-canned or even freshly stewed tomatoes with liquid.

CREAMY BUTTERNUT SOUP

Thick and velvety, this soup topped with chives and a drizzle of sour cream, looks as special as it tastes.
—Amanda Smith, Cincinnati, OH

Prep: 15 min. • **Cook:** 20 min.
Makes: 10 servings (2½ qt.)

- 1 medium butternut squash, peeled, seeded and cubed (about 6 cups)
- 3 medium potatoes (about 1 lb.), peeled and cubed
- 1 large onion, diced
- 2 chicken bouillon cubes
- 2 garlic cloves, minced
- 5 cups water
- Sour cream and minced fresh chives, optional

1. In a 6-qt. stockpot, combine first 6 ingredients; bring to a boil. Reduce heat; simmer, covered, until vegetables are tender, 15-20 minutes.
2. Puree the soup using an immersion blender. Or, cool slightly and puree soup in batches in a blender; return to pan and heat through. If desired, serve with sour cream and chives.
1 cup: 112 cal., 0 fat (0 sat. fat), 0 chol., 231mg sod., 27g carb. (5g sugars, 4g fiber), 3g pro.
Diabetic exchanges: 2 starch.

CHICKEN PESTO SANDWICHES

These easy sandwiches are great for game day! They're tasty, and also so easy to prep ahead and assemble later at the event.
—Colleen Sturma, Milwaukee, WI

Takes: 30 min. **Makes:** 6 servings

- 6 boneless skinless chicken breast halves (6 oz. each)
- ¾ cup prepared pesto, divided
- ½ tsp. salt
- ¼ tsp. pepper
- 1 jar (12 oz.) roasted sweet red peppers, drained
- 6 Ciabatta buns, split and toasted
- ¼ lb. fresh mozzarella cheese, cut into 6 slices

1. Flatten chicken to ¼-in. thickness. Spread 1 Tbsp. pesto over each chicken breast; sprinkle with salt and pepper. Grill the chicken, covered, over medium heat until no longer pink, 3-5 minutes on each side.
2. Spread 3 Tbsp. pesto over 6 slices of toast; layer with red peppers, chicken and cheese. Spread the remaining 3 Tbsp. pesto over remaining toast slices; place over top.
1 sandwich: 498 cal., 22g fat (6g sat. fat), 111mg chol., 1026mg sod., 27g carb. (6g sugars, 1g fiber), 43g pro.

CHICKEN PESTO SANDWICHES

BUFFALO CHICKEN WING SOUP

My husband and I really love buffalo chicken wings, so we created a soup with the same zippy flavor. Thick, creamy and comforting, it's very popular with our guests. Serve it with thick slices of bread. Start with a small amount of hot sauce, then add more if needed to suit your family's tastes.

—Pat Farmer, Falconer, New York

Prep: 5 min. • **Cook:** 4 hours
Makes: 8 servings.

- 5 cups 2% milk
- 3 cans (10¾ ounces each) condensed cream of chicken soup, undiluted
- 3 cups shredded cooked chicken (about 1 pound)
- 1 cup sour cream
- ¼ to ½ cup Louisiana-style hot sauce
- Optional: Sliced celery and additional hot sauce

In a 5-qt. slow cooker, mix the first 5 ingredients. Cook, covered, on low until heated through and the flavors are blended, 4-5 hours. If desired, top servings with celery and additional hot sauce.

1⅓ cups: 572 calories, 29g fat (11g saturated fat), 180mg cholesterol, 1308mg sodium, 18g carbohydrate (9g sugars, 2g fiber), 57g protein.

PRESSURE-COOKER
CAROLINA-STYLE
VINEGAR BBQ CHICKEN

PRESSURE-COOKER CAROLINA-STYLE VINEGAR BBQ CHICKEN

I live in Georgia but I appreciate the tangy, sweet and slightly spicy taste of Carolina vinegar chicken. Give it a try!

—Ramona Parris, Canton, GA

Takes: 25 min.
Makes: 6 servings

- 2 cups water
- 1 cup white vinegar
- ¼ cup sugar
- 1 Tbsp. reduced-sodium chicken base
- 1 tsp. crushed red pepper flakes
- ¾ tsp. salt
- 1½ lbs. boneless skinless chicken breasts
- 6 whole wheat hamburger buns, split, optional

1. In a 6-qt. electric pressure cooker, mix first 6 ingredients; add chicken. Lock lid and close the pressure-release valve. Adjust to pressure-cook on high for 5 minutes.

2. Allow the pressure to naturally release for 8 minutes, and then quick-release any remaining pressure.

3. Remove chicken and cool slightly. Reserve 1 cup cooking juices and discard remaining juices. Shred the chicken with 2 forks. Combine with reserved juices. If desired, serve chicken mixture on buns.

½ cup: 135 cal., 3g fat (1g sat. fat), 63mg chol., 228mg sod., 3g carb. (3g sugars, 0 fiber), 23g pro.
Diabetic exchanges: 3 lean meat.

CHIPOTLE BLT WRAPS

BLT sandwiches are so good, but they can make a lot of messy crumbs from the toasted bread. Since we also love wraps, I decided to make BLTs using tortillas instead. Warming the wraps a little makes them easy to work with.
—Darlene Brenden, Salem, OR

Takes: 15 min.
Makes: 4 servings

- 3 cups chopped romaine
- 2 plum tomatoes, finely chopped
- 8 bacon strips, cooked and crumbled
- ⅓ cup reduced-fat chipotle or regular mayonnaise
- 4 flour tortillas (8 in.), warmed

1. In a large bowl, combine romaine, tomatoes and bacon. Add mayonnaise; toss to coat.
2. Spoon about 1 cup romaine mixture down center of each tortilla. Fold bottom of tortilla over filling; fold both sides to close. Serve immediately.
1 wrap: 306 cal., 15g fat (4g sat. fat), 23mg chol., 689mg sod., 32g carb. (3g sugars, 3g fiber), 11g pro.

CHIPOTLE BLT WRAPS

GARLIC FENNEL BISQUE

TURKEY SAUSAGE, BUTTERNUT SQUASH & KALE SOUP

Kale and butternut squash are two of my favorite fall veggies. This recipe combines them into a warm and comforting soup. If you love sweet potatoes, sub them for the squash.

—Laura Koch, Lincoln, NE

Prep: 20 min. • **Cook:** 30 min.
Makes: 10 servings (2½ qt.)

- 1 pkg. (19½ oz.) Italian turkey sausage links, casings removed
- 1 medium butternut squash (about 3 lbs.), peeled and cubed
- 2 cartons (32 oz. each) reduced-sodium chicken broth
- 1 bunch kale, trimmed and coarsely chopped (about 16 cups)
- ½ cup shaved Parmesan cheese

1. In a stockpot, cook sausage over medium heat until no longer pink, breaking into crumbles, 8-10 minutes.
2. Add squash and broth; bring to a boil. Gradually stir in kale, allowing it to wilt slightly between additions. Return to a boil. Reduce heat; simmer, uncovered, until vegetables are tender, 15-20 minutes. Top servings with cheese.
1 cup: 163 cal., 5g fat (2g sat. fat), 23mg chol., 838mg sod., 20g carb. (5g sugars, 5g fiber), 13g pro.

GARLIC FENNEL BISQUE

I usually serve this soup in the spring as a wonderful side dish or first course. The fennel flavor is so refreshing.

—Janet Ondrich, Thamesville, ON

Prep: 30 min. • **Cook:** 40 min.
Makes: 14 servings

- 4 cups water
- 2½ cups half-and-half cream
- 24 garlic cloves, peeled and halved
- 3 medium fennel bulbs, cut into ½-in. pieces
- 2 Tbsp. chopped fennel fronds
- ½ tsp. salt
- ⅛ tsp. pepper
- ½ cup pine nuts, toasted

1. In a Dutch oven, bring the water, cream and garlic to a boil. Reduce heat; cover and simmer for 15 minutes or until garlic is very soft. Add the fennel and fennel fronds; cover and simmer 15 minutes longer or until fennel is very soft.
2. Cool slightly. In a blender, process soup in batches until blended. Return all to the pan. Season with salt and pepper; heat through. Sprinkle each serving with pine nuts.
½ cup: 108 cal., 7g fat (3g sat. fat), 21mg chol., 133mg sod., 8g carb. (2g sugars, 2g fiber), 4g pro.

TURKEY SAUSAGE, BUTTERNUT SQUASH & KALE SOUP

OPEN-FACED PEPPERONI SANDWICHES

OPEN-FACED PEPPERONI SANDWICHES

Between working full time, going to school and raising three children, finding time-saving recipes that my family actually enjoys is one of my biggest challenges. These quick little pizzas pack a huge amount of flavor.

—Amy Grim, Chillicothe, OH

Takes: 15 min. • **Makes:** 8 slices

- 1 pkg. (11¼ oz.) frozen garlic Texas toast
- ½ cup pizza sauce
- 1 pkg. (3½ oz.) sliced regular or turkey pepperoni
- 2 cups shredded part-skim mozzarella cheese

1. Preheat oven to 425°. Place Texas toast in a 15x10x1-in. baking pan. Bake 5 minutes.

2. Spread toast with pizza sauce; top with pepperoni and cheese. Bake until cheese is melted, about 4-5 minutes longer.

1 sandwich: 281 cal., 20g fat (8g sat. fat), 58mg chol., 610mg sod., 14g carb. (3g sugars, 1g fiber), 12g pro.

HAWAIIAN PULLED PORK LETTUCE WRAPS

We love this easy slow-cooker recipe on Sunday afternoons. It's equally comforting and light for lunch or dinner. We serve ours with sweet potato oven fries and roasted green beans.
—Arlene Rakoczy, Gilbert, AZ

Prep: 10 min. • **Cook:** 6 hours
Makes: 6 servings

- 1 boneless pork shoulder butt roast (3 to 4 lbs.)
- 1 tsp. rubbed sage
- 1 tsp. salt, divided
- ¼ tsp. pepper
- 1 can (20 oz.) unsweetened crushed pineapple, undrained
- 2 Tbsp. minced fresh gingerroot
- 18 Boston or Bibb lettuce leaves
- Thinly sliced green onions, optional

1. Rub roast with sage, ½ tsp. salt and pepper. Place in a 4- or 5-qt. slow cooker. Top with pineapple and ginger. Cook, covered, on low until meat is tender, 6-8 hours.

2. Remove roast; shred with 2 forks. Strain cooking juices. Reserve pineapple and 1 cup juices; discard remaining juices. Skim fat from reserved juices. Return the pork and cooking juices to slow cooker; stir in remaining ½ tsp. salt. Heat through. Serve in lettuce leaves with reserved pineapple and, if desired, green onions.

Freeze option: Freeze cooled meat mixture and juices in freezer containers. To use, partially thaw in the refrigerator overnight. Heat through in a saucepan, stirring occasionally; add water if necessary.

3 wraps: 430 cal., 23g fat (8g sat. fat), 135mg chol., 535mg sod., 16g carb. (14g sugars, 1g fiber), 39g pro.

TEST KITCHEN TIP
Sage and ginger flavor this mildly sweet pork dish. If you'd like yours sweeter, add a drizzle of honey to the pork mixture.

HAWAIIAN PULLED PORK LETTUCE WRAPS

GRILLED BEEF & BLUE CHEESE SANDWICHES

Roast beef, red onion and blue cheese really amp up this deluxe grilled sandwich. If you like a little heat, mix some horseradish into the spread.
—Bonnie Hawkins, Elkhorn, WI

Takes: 25 min.
Makes: 4 servings

- 2 oz. cream cheese, softened
- 2 oz. crumbled blue cheese
- 8 slices sourdough bread
- ¾ lb. thinly sliced deli roast beef
- ½ small red onion, thinly sliced
- ¼ cup olive oil

1. In a small bowl, mix cream cheese and blue cheese until blended. Spread over bread slices. Layer 4 of the slices with roast beef and onion; top with remaining bread slices.

2. Brush outsides of sandwiches with oil. In a large skillet, toast sandwiches over medium heat until golden brown, 4-5 minutes on each side.

1 sandwich: 471 cal., 27g fat (9g sat. fat), 72mg chol., 1021mg sod., 31g carb. (4g sugars, 1g fiber), 27g pro.

OPEN-FACED SALSA STEAK SANDWICHES

These open-faced steak sandwiches play up the popular combo of steak and garlic bread. The salsa, sour cream and garnish elevate it into quick, satisfying meal. Substitute chopped green onions or chives for the cilantro if desired.

—Arlene Erlbach, Morton Grove, IL

Takes: 25 min.
Makes: 4 servings

- 4 slices frozen garlic Texas toast
- 1 Tbsp. olive oil
- 1 beef top sirloin steak (1 lb.), thinly sliced
- 1½ cups salsa
- Sour cream and chopped fresh cilantro

1. Prepare garlic toast according to package directions.

2. Meanwhile, in a large skillet, heat oil over medium heat. Saute the steak until no longer pink, 3-5 minutes; drain. Stir in the salsa; cook and stir until heated through. Serve over toast. Top with sour cream and cilantro.

1 garlic toast with ¾ cup steak mixture: 375 cal., 16g fat (4g sat. fat), 52mg chol., 721mg sod., 27g carb. (5g sugars, 1g fiber), 29g pro.

OPEN-FACED SALSA STEAK SANDWICHES

SAUSAGE PEPPER SANDWICHES

SAUSAGE PEPPER SANDWICHES

Peppers and onions add fresh flavor to this sausage filling for sandwiches. It's simple to assemble, and it's always gobbled up quickly.

—Suzette Gessel, Albuquerque, NM

Prep: 15 min. • **Cook:** 3 hours
Makes: 6 servings

- 6 Italian sausage links (4 oz. each)
- 1 medium green pepper, cut into 1-in. pieces
- 1 large onion, cut into 1-in. pieces
- 1 can (8 oz.) tomato sauce
- 1/8 tsp. pepper
- 6 hoagie or submarine sandwich buns, split

1. In a large skillet, brown sausage links over medium heat. Cut into 1/2-in. slices; place in a 3-qt. slow cooker. Stir in green pepper, onion, tomato sauce and pepper.
2. Cover and cook on low for 3-4 hours or until sausage is no longer pink and vegetables are tender. Use a slotted spoon to serve on buns.
1 sandwich: 389 cal., 17g fat (7g sat. fat), 38mg chol., 965mg sod., 42g carb. (9g sugars, 3g fiber), 18g pro.

RAMEN BROCCOLI SOUP

RAMEN BROCCOLI SOUP

Cheese and garlic powder are the secret to this tasty and heartwarming soup. Loaded with noodles, it hits the spot on cool winter days.

—Luella Dirks, Emelle, AL

Takes: 20 min.
Makes: 7 servings

- 5 cups water
- 1 pkg. (16 oz.) frozen broccoli cuts
- 2 pkg. (3 oz. each) chicken ramen noodles
- 1/4 tsp. garlic powder
- 3 slices process American cheese, cut into strips

1. In a large saucepan, bring water to a boil. Add broccoli; return to a boil. Reduce heat; cover and simmer for 3 minutes. Return to a boil. Break the noodles into small pieces; add to water. Cook 3 minutes longer, stirring occasionally.
2. Remove from the heat. Add the garlic powder, cheese and contents of seasoning packets from the noodles; stir until the cheese is melted. Serve soup immediately.
1 cup: 150 cal., 6g fat (4g sat. fat), 6mg chol., 573mg sod., 20g carb. (2g sugars, 2g fiber), 5g pro.
Diabetic exchanges: 1 starch, 1 vegetable, 1 fat.

HEARTY CANNELLINI & SAUSAGE SOUP

Is there anything heartier than a soup full of sausage, creamy cannellini beans and hearty cabbage? I don't think so!
—Pauline White, El Cajon, CA

Takes: 30 min.
Makes: 6 servings

- 12 oz. beef summer or smoked sausage, cut into ½-in. pieces
- 4½ cups vegetable broth
- 2 cans (15 oz. each) cannellini beans, rinsed and drained
- 4 cups coarsely chopped Chinese or napa cabbage
- 3 green onions, chopped
- ¼ tsp. salt
- ¼ tsp. pepper

In a large saucepan, cook and stir the sausage over medium heat until lightly browned; drain. Add the remaining ingredients; bring to a boil. Reduce heat; simmer until the cabbage is tender and flavors are blended, 5-10 minutes.

1⅓ cups: 283 cal., 14g fat (5g sat. fat), 35mg chol., 1672mg sod., 24g carb. (3g sugars, 6g fiber), 15g pro.

CREAMY BUTTERNUT SOUP

Thick and velvety, this soup topped with chives and a drizzle of sour cream, looks as special as it tastes.
—Amanda Smith, Cincinnati, OH

Prep: 15 min. • **Cook:** 20 min.
Makes: 10 servings (2½ qt.)

- 1 medium butternut squash, peeled, seeded and cubed (about 6 cups)
- 3 medium potatoes (about 1 lb.), peeled and cubed
- 1 large onion, diced
- 2 chicken bouillon cubes
- 2 garlic cloves, minced
- 5 cups water
- Sour cream and minced fresh chives, optional

1. In a 6-qt. stockpot, combine first 6 ingredients; bring to a boil. Reduce heat; simmer, covered, until vegetables are tender, 15-20 minutes.

2. Puree the soup using an immersion blender. Or, cool slightly and puree the soup in batches in a blender; return to the pan and heat through. If desired, serve with sour cream and chives.

1 cup: 112 cal., 0 fat (0 sat. fat), 0 chol., 231mg sod., 27g carb. (5g sugars, 4g fiber), 3g pro.
Diabetic exchanges: 2 starch.

CREAMY BUTTERNUT SOUP

ITALIAN CHICKEN WRAPS

After enjoying a chicken wrap at a restaurant, I experimented at home to create something similar. My version is as fast as it is yummy.

—Cathy Hofflander, Adrian, MI

Takes: 25 min.
Makes: 6 servings

- 1 pkg. (16 oz.) frozen stir-fry vegetable blend
- 2 pkg. (6 oz. each) ready-to-use grilled chicken breast strips
- ½ cup fat-free Italian salad dressing
- 3 Tbsp. shredded Parmesan cheese
- 6 flour tortillas (8 in.), room temperature

In a large saucepan, cook the vegetables according to package directions; drain. Stir in the chicken, salad dressing and cheese; heat through. Spoon about ¾ cup down the center of each tortilla; roll up tightly.

1 serving: 290 cal., 6g fat (2g sat. fat), 40mg chol., 1129mg sod., 38g carb. (2g sugars, 3g fiber), 20g pro.

QUICK SOUTHWESTERN CHICKEN SOUP

QUICK SOUTHWESTERN CHICKEN SOUP

When I don't feel like going to the grocery store, the ingredients for this soup are always in my pantry! It's so easy and quick to make, and it tastes amazing!

—Rachel Hannah, Saraland, AL

Takes: 25 min.
Makes: 5 servings

- 2 cans (14½ oz. each) chicken broth
- 1 cup salsa
- 3 cups cubed cooked chicken
- 1 can (15 oz.) black beans, rinsed and drained
- 2 cups coarsely chopped fresh spinach

In a large saucepan, bring broth and salsa to a boil. Reduce heat. Add chicken and beans; heat through. Stir in spinach; cook until wilted. Serve immediately.

1½ cups: 253 cal., 4g fat (1g sat. fat), 81mg chol., 1140mg sod., 16g carb. (3g sugars, 4g fiber), 33g pro.

HEARTY VEGETABLE BEEF SOUP

My easy soup is packed with homemade flavor. Thanks to convenience products, it's perfect for a weeknight supper, but it would also make a tasty lunch on a snowy Saturday.

—Joanne Meehan, Shippensburg, PA

Takes: 30 min.
Makes: 8 servings (2½ qt.)

- 1 pkg. (17 oz.) refrigerated beef roast au jus
- 2 cans (14½ oz. each) Italian diced tomatoes, undrained
- 1 pkg. (16 oz.) frozen mixed vegetables
- 5½ cups water
- ¼ tsp. salt
- 1½ cups uncooked mini penne pasta

1. Shred beef with 2 forks; transfer to a Dutch oven. Add tomatoes, vegetables, water and salt. Bring to a boil. Stir in pasta. Reduce heat; simmer, uncovered, until flavors are blended and pasta is tender, at least 15 minutes.

1⅓ cups: 238 cal., 5g fat (2g sat. fat), 37mg chol., 705mg sod., 33g carb. (9g sugars, 4g fiber), 17g pro. **Diabetic exchanges:** 1 starch, 1 lean meat, 1 vegetable.

BARBECUED TURKEY CHILI

This so-simple chili takes just minutes to mix together, and the slow cooker does the rest. It's often requested by my friends and family when we all get together.
—Melissa Webb, Ellsworth, SD

Prep: 5 min. • **Cook:** 4 hours
Makes: 6 servings

- 1 can (16 oz.) kidney beans, rinsed and drained
- 1 can (16 oz.) hot chili beans, undrained
- 1 can (15 oz.) turkey chili with beans
- 1 can (14½ oz.) diced tomatoes, undrained
- ⅓ cup barbecue sauce

In a 3-qt. slow cooker, combine all of the ingredients. Cover and cook on high until heated through and the flavors are blended, about for 4 hours.
1 cup: 215 cal., 2g fat (1g sat. fat), 10mg chol., 936mg sod., 36g carb. (7g sugars, 10g fiber), 14g pro.

BARBECUED TURKEY CHILI

PICO DE GALLO
BLACK BEAN SOUP

PICO DE GALLO BLACK BEAN SOUP

Everyone at my table goes for this feel-good soup. It's quick when you're pressed for time and beats fast food, hands down. Serve it with tortilla chips or warm cornbread.
—Darlis Wilfer, West Bend, WI

Takes: 20 min.
Makes: 6 servings (about 2 qt.)

- 4 cans (15 oz. each) black beans, rinsed and drained
- 2 cups vegetable broth
- 2 cups pico de gallo
- ½ cup water
- 2 tsp. ground cumin
- Optional toppings: Chopped fresh cilantro and additional pico de gallo

1. In a Dutch oven, combine the first 5 ingredients; bring to a boil over medium heat, stirring occasionally. Reduce heat; simmer, uncovered, until vegetables in pico de gallo are softened, 5-7 minutes, stirring occasionally.
2. Puree the soup using an immersion blender, or cool soup slightly and puree in batches in a blender. Return to pan and heat through. Serve with the toppings as desired.
Freeze option: Freeze cooled soup in freezer containers. To use, partially thaw in refrigerator overnight. Heat through in a saucepan, stirring occasionally; add a little broth or water if necessary. Top as desired.

SPINACH FETA CROISSANTS

1¼ cups: 241 cal., 0 fat (0 sat. fat), 0 chol., 856mg sod., 44g carb. (4g sugars, 12g fiber), 14g pro.

TEST KITCHEN TIP
Black beans are naturally low in fat and high in fiber, protein and folate.

SPINACH FETA CROISSANTS

I had this sandwich in a cafe and added my own twist to spruce it up. It would be lovely for a shower, picnic or special occasion. Use mini croissants for smaller servings.
—Dolores Brigham, Inglewood, CA

Takes: 20 min.
Makes: 6 servings

- ½ cup Italian salad dressing
- 6 croissants, split
- 3 cups fresh baby spinach
- 4 plum tomatoes, thinly sliced
- 1 cup (4 oz.) crumbled feta cheese

Brush salad dressing over the cut sides of croissants. On the bottom halves, layer the spinach, tomatoes and feta cheese; replace tops.
1 serving: 363 cal., 23g fat (10g sat. fat), 48mg chol., 959mg sod., 30g carb. (4g sugars, 3g fiber), 9g pro.

PESTO GRILLED CHEESE SANDWICHES

My daughter always says that with my cooking, I make the ordinary better. That's what this recipe is all about: an old favorite with a fresh new twist. Pair it with your favorite soup for a satisfying meal.

—Arlene Reagan, Norristown, PA

Takes: 10 min.
Makes: 4 servings

- 8 slices walnut-raisin bread
- 3 to 4 Tbsp. prepared pesto
- 8 slices provolone and mozzarella cheese blend
- 8 slices tomato
- ¼ cup butter, softened

1. Spread 4 slices of bread with the pesto. Layer with cheese and tomato; top with the remaining bread. Butter the outsides of sandwiches.
2. In a large skillet over medium heat, toast the sandwiches until golden brown and the cheese is melted, 2-3 minutes on each side.
1 sandwich: 435 cal., 29g fat (14g sat. fat), 61mg chol., 739mg sod., 31g carb. (14g sugars, 3g fiber), 15g pro.

EFFORTLESS BROCCOLI SOUP

Thick, tasty and filled to the brim with fresh broccoli, this soup is easy to make and oh-so good for you.

—Betty Vaughn, Elkhart, IN

Takes: 30 min.
Makes: 2 servings

- ¼ cup chopped onion
- 2 Tbsp. butter
- 2 cups chopped fresh broccoli
- 1 can (14½ oz.) reduced-sodium chicken broth
- ½ tsp. garlic powder
- ¼ tsp. pepper
- ⅛ tsp. salt
- Sour cream, optional

1. In a large saucepan, saute onion in butter until tender. Add the broccoli, broth, garlic powder, pepper and salt. Bring to a boil. Reduce heat; cover and simmer until broccoli is tender, 10-12 minutes. Cool slightly.
2. In a blender, cover and process soup until smooth. Return to the pan and heat through. Garnish servings with sour cream if desired.
1 cup: 147 cal., 12g fat (7g sat. fat), 30mg chol., 840mg sod., 7g carb. (3g sugars, 3g fiber), 6g pro.

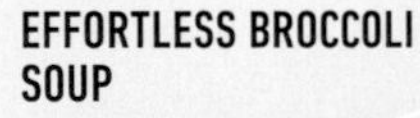

EFFORTLESS BROCCOLI SOUP

RIVEL SOUP

For years, I tried to figure out how my grandmother made her rivel soup. I discovered that it wasn't just something she came up with, but a prized heirloom recipe. Many families have their own special version.
—Kathy Kegley, Rural Retreat, VA

Takes: 10 min.
Makes: 6 servings

- 1 cup all-purpose flour
- ½ tsp. salt
- 1 large egg
- 4 cups 2% milk
- Minced fresh parsley and coarsely ground pepper

1. In a small bowl, combine flour and salt. Cut in egg with a fork until crumbly.
2. In a large saucepan, heat milk over medium heat until bubbles form around sides of pan. Gradually add flour mixture; bring to a gentle boil, stirring constantly. Cook and stir until rivels are cooked through, 1-2 minutes. Sprinkle servings with parsley and pepper.

¾ cup: 169 cal., 4g fat (2g sat. fat), 47mg chol., 290mg sod., 24g carb. (8g sugars, 1g fiber), 9g pro.

TEST KITCHEN TIP

Rivels are tiny dumpling-like bits often made of flour and egg. They are usually boiled right in the pot with the other soup ingredients. Common in Pennsylvania Dutch dishes, rivels are plump and slightly chewy.

MEDITERRANEAN
MEATBALL SANDWICHES

MEDITERRANEAN MEATBALL SANDWICHES

I grow onions, garlic and herbs, so that's what I use in these saucy sandwiches. Make patties or form the ground beef into meatballs instead.
—Alysha Braun, St. Catharines, ON

Takes: 25 min.
Makes: 4 servings

- 1 small onion, finely chopped
- ¼ cup minced fresh parsley
- ½ tsp. salt
- ¼ tsp. pepper
- 1 lb. ground beef
- 4 whole pita breads, warmed
- Refrigerated tzatziki sauce
- Optional toppings: sliced tomato, chopped red onion and shredded lettuce

1. In a large bowl, combine the onion, parsley, salt and pepper. Add beef and mix lightly but thoroughly. Shape into four 4x2-in. oblong patties.

2. Grill patties, covered, over medium heat or broil 4 in. from heat until a thermometer reads 160°, 4-6 minutes on each side. Serve on pitas with tzatziki sauce and toppings as desired.

1 serving: 379 cal., 14g fat (5g sat. fat), 70mg chol., 682mg sod., 35g carb. (2g sugars, 2g fiber), 26g pro.

SUCCULENT STRAWBERRY SOUP

This cool creamy fruit soup makes a perfect summertime treat for family and friends. The strawberry base with a hint of orange appeals to all palates!
—Paula Pelis, Lenhartsville, PA

Prep: 30 min. + chilling
Makes: 4 servings

- 2 qt. fresh strawberries, divided
- ½ cup water
- 5 Tbsp. sugar
- 1 Tbsp. all-purpose flour
- 1 tsp. grated orange zest
- 1 cup heavy whipping cream
- Fresh mint and additional strawberries, optional

1. Mash half the strawberries with a potato masher or fork.
2. In a blender, combine the remaining strawberries, water, sugar, flour and orange zest; process until smooth. Pour into a 2-qt. saucepan. Bring to a boil over medium heat; boil 2 minutes, stirring constantly. Add the mashed strawberries. Reduce the heat and simmer, uncovered, for 10 minutes, stirring constantly. Chill for at least 1 hour.
3. Stir in cream. Cover and chill overnight. Serve with mint and strawberries if desired.
1 cup: 360 cal., 23g fat (14g sat. fat), 82mg chol., 26mg sod., 39g carb. (30g sugars, 7g fiber), 3g pro.

SUCCULENT STRAWBERRY SOUP

SWEET & TANGY
PULLED PORK

SWEET & TANGY PULLED PORK

The slow cooker makes these sandwiches a convenient option for busy weeknights. The apricot preserves lend a sweet flavor to the pork.
—Megan Klimkewicz, Kaiser, MO

Prep: 15 min. • **Cook:** 8 hours
Makes: 12 servings

- 1 jar (18 oz.) apricot preserves
- 1 large onion, chopped
- 2 Tbsp. reduced-sodium soy sauce
- 2 Tbsp. Dijon mustard
- 1 boneless pork shoulder butt roast (3 to 4 lbs.)
- Hamburger buns, split, optional

1. Mix first 4 ingredients. Place roast in a 4- or 5-qt. slow cooker; top with the preserves mixture. Cook, covered, on low until meat is tender, 8-10 hours.
2. Remove pork from the slow cooker. Skim fat from cooking juices. Shred pork with 2 forks; return to slow cooker and heat through. If desired, serve on hamburger buns.
½ cup pork mixture: 296 cal., 11g fat (4g sat. fat), 67mg chol., 243mg sod., 29g carb. (19g sugars, 0 fiber), 20g pro. **Diabetic exchanges:** 3 lean meat, 2 starch.

SMOKY GOUDA & CHICKEN SANDWICHES

SMOKY GOUDA & CHICKEN SANDWICHES

Here's a hearty, hot, delectable sandwich to take along on a picnic or to enjoy for a low-key dinner. Ready-to-eat rotisserie chicken makes it quick.
—Nancy Mock, Colchester, VT

Takes: 20 min.
Makes: 4 servings

- ¼ cup garlic-herb mayonnaise, divided
- 8 slices country white bread (½ in. thick), toasted
- 2 cups shredded rotisserie chicken
- ¼ tsp. salt
- ⅛ tsp. pepper
- 2 small peaches or medium plums, thinly sliced
- 4 slices smoked Gouda cheese

1. Preheat broiler. Spread 2 Tbsp. mayonnaise over 4 slices toast; place on a foil-lined baking sheet. Arrange chicken over the top; sprinkle with the salt and pepper. Layer with the peaches and cheese.
2. Broil 3-4 in. from heat until cheese is melted, 2-3 minutes. Spread remaining mayonnaise over remaining toast; place over the tops.
1 sandwich: 352 cal., 17g fat (7g sat. fat), 100mg chol., 678mg sod., 18g carb. (5g sugars, 1g fiber), 30g pro.

CONTEST-WINNING ROASTED TOMATO SOUP

Just before the first frost of the season, we gather up all of the tomatoes from my mom's garden to create this flavorful soup. Although it sounds like a lot of garlic, when it's roasted, the garlic becomes mellow and almost sweet. We serve this soup with toasted bread spread with pesto.

—Kaitlyn Lerdahl, Madison, WI

Prep: 25 min. • **Cook:** 40 min.
Makes: 6 servings

- 15 large tomatoes (5 lbs.), seeded and quartered
- ¼ cup plus 2 Tbsp. canola oil, divided
- 8 garlic cloves, minced
- 1 large onion, chopped
- 2 cups water
- 1 tsp. salt
- ½ tsp. crushed red pepper flakes, optional
- ½ cup heavy whipping cream
- Fresh basil leaves, optional

1. Preheat oven to 400°. Place the tomatoes in a greased 15x10x1-in. baking pan. Combine ¼ cup oil and garlic; drizzle over tomatoes. Toss to coat. Bake until softened, 15-20 minutes, stirring occasionally. Remove and discard skins.

2. Meanwhile, in a Dutch oven, saute onion in remaining 2 Tbsp. oil until tender. Add tomatoes, water, salt and, if desired, pepper flakes. Bring to a boil. Reduce heat; cover and simmer until flavors are blended, about 30 minutes. Cool slightly.

3. In a blender, process soup in batches until smooth. Return to pan. Stir in cream and heat through. Sprinkle with the basil if desired.

Freeze option: Cool soup and transfer to freezer containers. Freeze up to 3 months. To use, thaw in the refrigerator overnight. Place in a large saucepan; heat through. Garnish with the basil if desired.

1 cup: 276 cal., 22g fat (6g sat. fat), 27mg chol., 421mg sod., 19g carb. (11g sugars, 5g fiber), 4g pro.

CONTEST-WINNING ROASTED TOMATO SOUP

★★★★★ READER REVIEW

"I have a gluten and corn allergy, and I could not find any good soups. This is the best soup I've made so far, and it's now my favorite! Very good on a cold gloomy day!"

—MARIABAUTISTA, TASTEOFHOME.COM

PORTOBELLO-GOUDA GRILLED SANDWICHES

PORTOBELLO-GOUDA GRILLED SANDWICHES

Take a simple grilled cheese sandwich to the next level with portobello mushrooms and Gouda cheese. Whip up a side of tomato soup, and lunch is ready to serve!

—Sheryl Bergman, Shady Side, MD

Takes: 20 min.
Makes: 2 servings

- 1 cup sliced baby portobello mushrooms
- 1 Tbsp. plus 4 tsp. butter, divided
- 4 oz. smoked Gouda cheese, sliced
- 4 slices rye bread
- 1 plum tomato, sliced

1. In a large skillet, saute the mushrooms in 1 Tbsp. butter until tender. Place cheese on 2 bread slices; top with the mushrooms, tomato and the remaining bread. Spread the outsides of sandwiches with the remaining 4 tsp. butter.

2. In a small skillet over medium heat, toast sandwiches until the cheese is melted, 2-3 minutes on each side.

1 sandwich: 498 cal., 31g fat (19g sat. fat), 100mg chol., 984mg sod., 35g carb. (5g sugars, 5g fiber), 21g pro.

CREAM OF BUTTERNUT SQUASH SOUP

CREAM OF BUTTERNUT SQUASH SOUP

Butternut squash makes a luscious soup for chilly days when you need warmth from the inside out. We add potatoes and a touch of chicken soup mix to boost it a bit.

—Tiffany Smith, Cincinnati, OH

Prep: 15 min. • **Cook:** 40 min.
Makes: 6 servings (1½ qt.)

- 4 cups cubed peeled butternut squash (about 1 lb.)
- 2 medium potatoes (about 1 lb.), peeled and cubed
- 1 medium onion, chopped
- 4 cups water
- 1 carton (2½ oz.) chicken noodle soup mix
- 1 cup half-and-half cream
- ¼ tsp. salt
- ¼ tsp. pepper
- Chopped fresh parsley, optional

1. Place first 5 ingredients in a large saucepan; bring to a boil. Reduce heat; simmer, covered, until squash and potatoes are tender, 40-45 minutes.

2. Puree the soup using an immersion blender. Or, cool soup slightly and puree in batches in a blender; return to pan. Stir in cream, salt and pepper; heat through. If desired, sprinkle servings with parsley.

1 cup: 192 cal., 5g fat (3g sat. fat), 28mg chol., 676mg sod., 33g carb. (6g sugars, 3g fiber), 5g pro.

WAFFLE-IRON PIZZA SANDWICHES

These little pizza pockets are a fun mashup using the waffle iron. Try your favorite toppings or even breakfast fillings like ham and eggs.

—Amy Lents, Grand Forks, ND

Takes: 30 min.
Makes: 4 servings

- 1 pkg. (16.3 oz.) large refrigerated buttermilk biscuits
- 1 cup shredded part-skim mozzarella cheese
- 24 slices turkey pepperoni (about 1½ oz.)
- 2 ready-to-serve fully cooked bacon strips, chopped
- Pizza sauce, warmed

1. Roll or press biscuits to fit waffle iron. On 1 biscuit, place ¼ cup cheese, 6 slices pepperoni and 1 scant Tbsp. chopped bacon to within ½ in. of edges. Top with a second biscuit, folding bottom edge over top edge and pressing to seal completely.
2. Bake in a preheated waffle iron according to manufacturer's directions until golden brown, 4-5 minutes. Repeat with the remaining ingredients. Serve with pizza sauce.
1 pizza: 461 cal., 21g fat (8g sat. fat), 28mg chol., 1650mg sod., 50g carb. (5g sugars, 2g fiber), 19g pro.

WAFFLE-IRON PIZZA SANDWICHES

BREAKFAST FOR DINNER

BREAKFAST BREAD PUDDING
P. 238

1

2

3

4

5

JAZZ UP DINNER WITH ONE OF THESE EYE-OPENING ENTREES.

BRUNCH-STYLE PORTOBELLO MUSHROOMS

BANANA PANCAKE FOR ONE

Get a delicious start to the day with this tender and hearty pancake. Try coconut or almond extract in place of the vanilla for a fun change of pace.

—Carmen Bolar, Bronx, NY

Takes: 15 min. • **Makes:** 1 pancake

- ¼ cup plus 1 Tbsp. all-purpose flour
- ½ tsp. baking powder
- 1 medium ripe banana, mashed
- 1 large egg, lightly beaten
- ½ tsp. vanilla extract
- Maple syrup, optional

1. In a small bowl, combine flour and baking powder. Combine banana, egg, and vanilla; stir into dry ingredients just until moistened.
2. Pour batter onto a hot griddle coated with cooking spray; turn when bubbles form on top and pancake is golden brown on 1 side. Cook until the second side is golden brown. Serve with syrup and additional bananas if desired.

1 serving: 325 cal., 6g fat (2g sat. fat), 186mg chol., 313mg sod., 57g carb. (15g sugars, 4g fiber), 12g pro.

BRUNCH-STYLE PORTOBELLO MUSHROOMS

I've always loved portobellos for their stuffability. I combined my favorite ingredients for this rich, savory main dish that's wonderful for breakfast, brunch or even dinner!

—Sylvia Waldsmith, Rockton, IL

Takes: 30 min.
Makes: 4 servings

- 4 large portobello mushrooms, stems removed
- 2 pkg. (10 oz. each) frozen creamed spinach, thawed
- 4 large eggs
- ¼ cup shredded Gouda cheese
- ½ cup crumbled cooked bacon
- Salt and pepper, optional

1. Place mushrooms, stem side up, in an ungreased 15x10x1-in. baking pan. Spoon spinach onto mushrooms, building up sides. Carefully crack an egg into the center of each mushroom; sprinkle with cheese and bacon.
2. Bake mushrooms at 375° for 18-20 minutes or until the eggs are set. Sprinkle with salt and pepper if desired.

1 serving: 265 cal., 12g fat (5g sat. fat), 204mg chol., 1058mg sod., 17g carb. (7g sugars, 1g fiber), 20g pro.

BANANA PANCAKE FOR ONE

EGGS BENEDICT BAKED POTATOES

This is a new way to prepare breakfast potatoes! This baked dish would be "eggs-cellent" for brunch or a breakfast-for-dinner evening!

—Becky Carver, North Royalton, OH

Prep: 20 min. • **Bake:** 50 min.
Makes: 4 servings

- 4 large baking potatoes
- 4 large eggs
- ½ tsp. salt
- ½ tsp. pepper
- 8 slices halved Canadian bacon, warmed
- ¼ cup prepared hollandaise sauce
- Minced fresh parsley, optional

1. Preheat the oven to 400°. Scrub the potatoes; pierce the potatoes several times with a fork. Bake until tender, 50-75 minutes.

2. Meanwhile, place 2-3 in. of water in a large saucepan or skillet with high sides. Bring to a boil; adjust heat to maintain a gentle simmer. Break cold eggs, 1 at a time, into a small bowl; holding bowl close to surface of water, slip egg into water.

3. Cook, uncovered, until whites are completely set and yolks begin to thicken but are not hard, 3-5 minutes. Using a slotted spoon, lift eggs out of water. With a sharp knife, cut an "X" in each potato. Fluff pulp with a fork; season with salt and pepper. Top potatoes with Canadian bacon, poached eggs and hollandaise sauce. If desired, sprinkle with minced parsley.

1 stuffed potato: 444 cal., 11g fat (5g sat. fat), 212mg chol., 535mg sod., 66g carb. (4g sugars, 8g fiber), 20g pro.

EGGS BENEDICT BAKED POTATOES

TEST KITCHEN TIP
Dress up these potatoes by placing cooked shrimp over the Canadian bacon before layering on the rest of the items.

CREAM CHEESE & CHIVE OMELET

The first bite of creamy filling lets you know this isn't any old omelet. Make it once, and we suspect you'll be fixing it often.
—Anne Troise, Manalapan, NJ

Takes: 15 min.
Makes: 2 servings

- 1 Tbsp. olive oil
- 4 large eggs
- 2 Tbsp. minced chives
- 2 Tbsp. water
- ⅛ tsp. salt
- ⅛ tsp. pepper
- 2 oz. cream cheese, cubed
- Salsa

1. In a large nonstick skillet, heat the oil over medium-high heat. Whisk the eggs, chives, water, salt and pepper. Add egg mixture to skillet (mixture should set immediately at edges).

2. As eggs set, push cooked edges toward the center, letting the uncooked portion flow underneath. When the eggs are set, sprinkle cream cheese on 1 side; fold other side over filling. Slide omelet onto a plate; cut in half. Serve with salsa.

½ omelet: 305 cal., 27g fat (10g sat. fat), 455mg chol., 374mg sod., 2g carb. (1g sugars, 0 fiber), 15g pro.

LIGHT & CRISPY WAFFLES

Club soda gives these crisp waffles a light, fluffy texture. With only four ingredients, homemade waffles can't get much easier than this!
—*Taste of Home* Test Kitchen

Takes: 20 min.
Makes: 12 waffles

- 2 cups biscuit/baking mix
- 2 large eggs, room temperature, lightly beaten
- ½ cup canola oil
- 1 cup club soda

1. In a large bowl, combine the biscuit mix, eggs and oil. Add club soda and stir until smooth.
2. Bake in a preheated waffle iron according to manufacturer's directions until golden brown.

Freeze option: Cool the waffles on wire racks. Freeze cooled waffles between layers of waxed paper in freezer containers. To use, reheat the waffles in a toaster on medium setting. Or, microwave each waffle on high for 30-60 seconds or until the waffle is heated through.

2 waffles: 348 cal., 26g fat (4g sat. fat), 71mg chol., 533mg sod., 25g carb. (1g sugars, 1g fiber), 5g pro.

TEST KITCHEN TIP
Jazz up these waffles by adding some snipped chives to the batter.

HASH BROWN BREAKFAST CASSEROLE

This savory, scrumptious recipe uses egg substitute for lower fat and cholesterol. Serve with fresh fruit for a morning meal that will keep your family satisfied.

—Cindy Schneider, Sarasota, FL

Prep: 10 min. • **Bake:** 40 min.
Makes: 4 servings

- 4 cups frozen shredded hash brown potatoes, thawed
- 1½ cups egg substitute
- 1 cup finely chopped cooked chicken breast
- ½ tsp. garlic powder
- ½ tsp. pepper
- ¾ cup shredded reduced-fat cheddar cheese

1. Preheat the oven to 350°. In a large bowl, combine the hash browns, egg substitute, chicken, garlic powder and pepper. Transfer to a greased 8-in. square baking dish; sprinkle with the cheese.
2. Bake, uncovered, until a knife inserted in the center comes out clean, 40-45 minutes. Let stand for 5 minutes before serving.

1 piece: 223 cal., 6g fat (3g sat. fat), 42mg chol., 353mg sod., 16g carb. (2g sugars, 1g fiber), 27g pro. **Diabetic exchanges:** 3 lean meat, 1 starch.

HASH BROWN BREAKFAST CASSEROLE

BAKED EGG &
STUFFING CUPS

BAKED EGG & STUFFING CUPS

Save any leftover stuffing to make shells for holding baked eggs. This is a hearty entree that always fill us up!
—Karen Deaver, Babylon, NY

Prep: 10 min. • **Bake:** 25 min.
Makes: 4 servings

- 1 cup cooked stuffing
- 4 large eggs
- ¼ tsp. salt
- ¼ tsp. pepper
- Minced fresh sage, optional

1. Preheat oven to 325°. Press stuffing into 4 greased 4-oz. ramekins, forming wells in centers. Break and slip an egg into center of each dish; sprinkle with salt and pepper.
2. Place ramekins on a baking sheet. Bake 25-30 minutes or until egg whites are completely set and yolks begin to thicken but are not hard. If desired, sprinkle with sage.

1 serving: 169 cal., 11g fat (3g sat. fat), 186mg chol., 458mg sod., 10g carb. (1g sugars, 0 fiber), 8g pro.

PRESSURE-COOKER MAPLE FRENCH TOAST

PRESSURE-COOKER MAPLE FRENCH TOAST

My family and friends all love it when I make this scrumptious French toast. It's so delicious and easy!
—Cindy Steffen, Cedarburg, WI

Prep: 10 min. + standing
Cook: 20 min. + releasing
Makes: 4 servings

- 6 cups cubed bread (about 6 oz.)
- 4 oz. cream cheese, cubed
- 4 large eggs
- ½ cup 2% milk
- ¼ cup maple syrup
- Additional maple syrup

1. Arrange half of the bread cubes in a greased 1½-qt. baking dish. Top with the cream cheese and remaining bread. In a large bowl, whisk eggs, milk and syrup; pour over bread. Let stand 30 minutes.
2. Place trivet insert and 1 cup water in a 6-qt. electric pressure cooker. Cover baking dish with foil. Fold an 18x12-in. piece of foil lengthwise into thirds, making a sling. Use sling to lower dish into pressure cooker. Lock the lid; close pressure-release valve. Adjust to pressure-cook on high for 20 minutes.
3. Allow pressure to naturally release for 10 minutes, then quick-release any remaining pressure. Remove lid; using sling, carefully remove baking dish. Serve with syrup.

1 cup: 378 cal., 17g fat (8g sat. fat), 217mg chol., 434mg sod., 43g carb. (18g sugars, 1g fiber), 14g pro.

PRONTO POTATO PANCAKES

PRONTO POTATO PANCAKES

Pancakes aren't just for breakfast! You can also serve them as a side dish with any meat. We like them with applesauce on top.

—Darlene Brenden, Salem, OR

Takes: 30 min.
Makes: 8 pancakes

- 2 large eggs, room temperature
- 1 small onion, halved
- 2 medium potatoes, peeled and cut into 1-in. cubes
- 2 to 4 Tbsp. all-purpose flour
- ½ tsp. salt
- ⅛ tsp. cayenne pepper
- 4 to 6 Tbsp. canola oil
- Applesauce, optional

1. Place eggs and onion in a blender; cover and process until blended. Add potatoes; cover and process until finely chopped. Transfer to a small bowl. Stir in the flour, salt and cayenne.
2. Heat 2 Tbsp. oil in a large cast-iron or other heavy skillet over medium heat. Drop batter by ¼ cupfuls into oil. Fry in batches until golden brown on both sides, using remaining oil as needed. Drain pancakes on paper towels. If desired, serve with applesauce.

2 pancakes: 263 cal., 17g fat (2g sat. fat), 93mg chol., 338mg sod., 23g carb. (2g sugars, 3g fiber), 6g pro.

HAM & BROCCOLI FRITTATA

With just a few ingredients, this cheesy frittata is a breeze to make. It's sure to become a new family favorite.

—Annie Rundle, Muskego, WI

Takes: 30 min.
Makes: 4 servings

- 6 large eggs
- ¼ tsp. pepper
- Dash salt
- 1¼ cups shredded Swiss cheese, divided
- 1 cup cubed fully cooked ham
- 1 Tbsp. butter
- 1 cup chopped fresh broccoli

HAM & BROCCOLI FRITTATA

1. Preheat broiler. In a bowl, whisk eggs, pepper and salt. Stir in 1 cup cheese and ham.
2. In a 10-in. ovenproof skillet, heat butter over medium-high heat. Add broccoli; cook and stir until tender. Reduce heat to low; pour in egg mixture. Cook, covered, 4-6 minutes or until nearly set. Sprinkle with remaining cheese.
3. Broil 3-4 in. from heat 2-3 minutes or until eggs are completely set. Let stand 5 minutes. Cut into wedges.

1 wedge: 321 cal., 23g fat (11g sat. fat), 374mg chol., 665mg sod., 4g carb. (2g sugars, 1g fiber), 26g pro.

HOT JAM BREAKFAST SANDWICHES

These sweet bites give a new meaning to grilled sandwiches. The combination of flavors are guaranteed to appeal to just about everyone.

—Gloria Jarrett, Loveland, OH

Takes: 20 min.
Makes: 6 servings

- ¼ cup butter
- ¼ cup sweetened shredded coconut
- ½ cup apricot jam
- ½ tsp. ground cinnamon
- 12 slices raisin bread

In a bowl, mix butter and coconut; stir in jam and cinnamon. Spread between slices of bread. Grill on a greased skillet until golden brown on both sides.

1 sandwich: 292 cal., 10g fat (6g sat. fat), 20mg chol., 222mg sod., 49g carb. (19g sugars, 4g fiber), 6g pro.

HOT & SPICY OMELET

HOT & SPICY OMELET

Red pepper flakes add plenty of fiery zip to this omelet. It's a favorite at our house—for breakfast, brunch or supper. We like it alongside sausage or bacon, home fries and oven-fresh biscuits.
—Dixie Terry, Goreville, IL

Takes: 15 min.
Makes: 4 servings

- 1 Tbsp. butter
- 1 Tbsp. canola oil
- 8 large eggs
- 2 Tbsp. water
- 4 garlic cloves, minced
- ½ tsp. salt
- ¼ tsp. pepper
- ¼ tsp. crushed red pepper flakes

1. In a large nonstick skillet, melt butter and oil over medium-high heat. Whisk eggs, water, garlic, salt and pepper. Add egg mixture to skillet (mixture should set immediately at edges).
2. As eggs set, push the cooked edges toward the center, letting the uncooked portion flow underneath. When the eggs are set; fold in half. Invert omelet onto a plate to serve. Sprinkle with red pepper flakes.

1 piece: 209 cal., 16g fat (5g sat. fat), 433mg chol., 451mg sod., 2g carb. (1g sugars, 0 fiber), 13g pro.

EASY GINGERBREAD PANCAKES

Simple yet scrumptious, these taste more like cake than pancakes. When I want to eat lighter, I top them with a little bit of applesauce.
—Trina Stewart, Yacolt, WA

Prep: 5 min. • **Cook:** 5 min./batch
Makes: 12 pancakes

- 2 cups complete pancake mix
- 4 tsp. molasses
- ½ tsp. ground cinnamon
- ½ tsp. ground ginger
- ⅛ tsp. ground cloves
- 1½ cups water
- Maple syrup, optional

1. In a small bowl, combine the pancake mix, molasses, cinnamon, ginger and cloves. Stir in water just until dry ingredients are moistened.
2. Pour batter by ¼ cupfuls onto a greased hot griddle; turn when bubbles form on top. Cook until the second side is golden brown. Serve with syrup if desired.

3 pancakes: 248 al., 2g fat (0 sat. fat), 0 chol., 972mg sod., 54g carb. (10g sugars, 1g fiber), 5g pro.

★★★★★ **READER REVIEW**

"Delicious! Made these for Christmas Eve breakfast. The family loved them especially with whipping cream! So easy with a mix!"
—GARY543, TASTEOFHOME.COM

CHEESY HAM & POTATO PACKET

I found the technique for grilling ham, potatoes and cheese in foil packets and changed up some ingredients to suit our tastes. I love that this great meal doesn't heat up the entire kitchen.

—Molly Bishop, McClure, PA

Takes: 30 min.
Makes: 4 servings

- 1½ lbs. medium red potatoes, halved and thinly sliced
- 1 medium green pepper, chopped
- 1 medium onion, chopped
- ¼ tsp. pepper
- 2 cups cubed deli ham
- 1 cup shredded cheddar cheese

1. In a large bowl, toss potatoes with green pepper, onion and pepper; place in center of a greased 24x18-in. piece of heavy-duty foil. Fold the foil around vegetables and crimp edges to seal.
2. Grill, covered, over medium heat 15-20 minutes or until potatoes are tender. Remove from grill. Open foil carefully to allow steam to escape. Add the ham; sprinkle with cheese. Grill the opened packet, covered, 2-4 minutes longer or until cheese is melted.

1½ cups: 341 cal., 13 g fat (6 g sat. fat), 70 mg chol., 1040 mg sod., 32 g carb. (4 g sugars, 4 g fiber), 26 g pro.

BREAKFAST BREAD PUDDING

I assemble this dish the day before our grandchildren visit. It gives me more time for fun with them instead of cooking!

—Alma Andrews, Live Oak, FL

Prep: 10 min. + chilling
Bake: 40 min. • **Makes:** 8 servings

- 12 slices white bread
- 1 pkg. (8 oz.) cream cheese, cubed
- 12 large eggs
- 2 cups whole milk
- ⅓ cup maple syrup
- ¼ tsp. salt

1. Remove and discard crusts from bread; cut bread into cubes. Toss lightly with cream cheese cubes; place cubes in a greased 13x9-in. baking pan. In a large bowl, beat eggs. Add milk, syrup and salt; mix well. Pour over bread mixture. Cover and refrigerate 8 hours or overnight.
2. Remove the refrigerator 30 minutes before baking. Preheat oven to 375°. Bake, uncovered, until a knife inserted in the center comes out clean, 40-45 minutes. Let stand 5 minutes before cutting.

1 piece: 383 cal., 21g fat (10g sat. fat), 359mg chol., 485mg sod., 32g carb. (14g sugars, 1g fiber), 17g pro.

CHEESY HAM & POTATO PACKET

SAUSAGE & GRAVY BISCUIT POCKETS

I love sausage gravy and biscuits, so I thought it would be a fabulous idea to make them portable for an easy on-the-go option.

—Stephanie Matthews, Tempe, AZ

Prep: 20 min. + cooling
Bake: 15 min.
Makes: 16 servings

- 1 lb. bulk pork sausage
- 2 Tbsp. butter
- ½ cup all-purpose flour
- ½ tsp. salt
- ½ tsp. pepper
- 4 cups 2% milk
- 2 tubes (16.3 oz. each) large refrigerated buttermilk biscuits

1. In a large skillet, cook sausage over medium heat until no longer pink, 3-5 minutes, breaking into crumbles. Add butter; heat until melted. Add flour, salt and pepper; cook and stir until blended. Gradually add milk, stirring constantly. Bring to a boil; cook and stir until thickened, about 3 minutes. Remove from heat; cool to room temperature, about 25 minutes.
2. Preheat oven to 400°. On a lightly floured surface, pat or roll each biscuit into a 6-in. circle. Spoon ½ cup gravy mixture over half of each circle to within ½ in. of edge. Wet edge and fold dough over filling; press edge with a fork to seal.
3. Place on an ungreased baking sheet. Bake until golden brown, 12-14 minutes.

Freeze option: Cover and freeze unbaked pockets on a waxed paper-lined baking sheet until firm. Transfer pockets to freezer containers; return to freezer. To use, bake the pockets on an ungreased baking sheet in a preheated 400° oven until golden brown and heated through, 12-14 minutes. If desired, brush with additional melted butter.

1 pocket: 313 cal., 17g fat (6g sat. fat), 28mg chol., 946mg sod., 31g carb. (6g sugars, 1g fiber), 10g pro.

SAUSAGE & GRAVY BISCUIT POCKETS

BLUEBERRY MUFFIN FRENCH TOAST

BLUEBERRY MUFFIN FRENCH TOAST

My 13-year-old daughter and her friends asked for French toast at a sleepover, but we were out of bread. I used muffins instead, and they loved it. Double or triple this recipe for a brunch.

—Bonnie Geavaras-Bootz, Chandler, AZ

Takes: 25 min.
Makes: 6 servings

- 4 day-old jumbo blueberry muffins
- 3 large eggs
- ¾ cup refrigerated French vanilla nondairy creamer
- ¼ tsp. ground cinnamon
- 3 Tbsp. butter
- Confectioners' sugar, optional

1. Trim rounded tops off muffins (save for another use). Cut remaining muffins crosswise into ½-in. slices.

2. In a shallow bowl, whisk eggs, creamer and cinnamon. In a large skillet, heat butter over medium heat. Dip both sides of muffin slices in egg mixture. Place in skillet; toast 2-3 minutes on each side or until golden brown. If desired, dust with confectioners' sugar.

2 pieces: 529 cal., 27g fat (7g sat. fat), 159mg chol., 563mg sod., 63g carb. (41g sugars, 1g fiber), 9g pro.

NUTTY WAFFLE SANDWICHES

How about this for a change-of-pace meal? You can't go wrong with peanut butter and Nutella, but the secret here is using really juicy strawberries. Never tried Nutella? Look for the hazelnut-flavored spread near the peanut butter at the grocery store.

—Frances Pietsch, Flower Mound, TX

Takes: 15 min.
Makes: 4 servings

- 8 frozen multigrain waffles
- ½ cup Nutella
- 2 medium bananas, sliced
- 1 cup sliced fresh strawberries
- ½ cup peanut butter

Toast waffles according to package directions. Spread 4 waffles with Nutella. Layer with bananas and strawberries. Spread remaining waffles with peanut butter; place over top.

1 sandwich: 600 cal., 32g fat (6g sat. fat), 0 chol., 555mg sod., 75g carb. (34g sugars, 10g fiber), 16g pro.

HEARTY SAUSAGE & HASH BROWNS

Turn frozen hash browns into a satisfying supper by adding smoked sausage and green peppers. It's a simple meal-in-one that works any time of day.

—Violet Beard, Marshall, IL

Takes: 30 min.
Makes: 3 servings

- 4 cups frozen cubed hash brown potatoes
- ¼ cup chopped green pepper
- ⅓ cup canola oil
- ¼ lb. smoked sausage, halved lengthwise and cut into ¼-in. slices
- 3 slices American cheese

In a large skillet, cook potatoes and pepper in oil over medium heat until potatoes are golden brown. Stir in sausage; heat through. Remove from heat; top with cheese. Cover and let stand for 5 minutes or until cheese is melted.

1 cup: 477 cal., 39g fat (11g sat. fat), 39mg chol., 695mg sod., 21g carb. (3g sugars, 2g fiber), 12g pro.

AIR-FRYER BACON EGG CUPS

These adorable cups are a fresh take on a classic combo. I originally baked these, but they're amazing in the air fryer.
—Carol Forcum, Marion, IL

Prep: 20 min. • **Cook:** 15 min.
Makes: 2 servings

- 4 bacon strips
- 4 large eggs
- ⅓ cup half-and-half cream
- ⅛ tsp. pepper
- ½ cup shredded cheddar cheese
- 2 green onions, chopped

1. In a small skillet, cook bacon over medium heat until cooked but not crisp. Remove to paper towels to drain; keep warm.
2. Preheat air fryer to 350°. In a small bowl, whisk 2 eggs, cream and pepper. Wrap 2 bacon strips around the inside edge of each of two 8-oz. ramekins or custard cups coated with cooking spray.
3. Sprinkle ramekins with half the cheese and onions. Divide egg mixture between ramekins. Break 1 remaining egg into each ramekin. Sprinkle with the remaining cheese and onions. Place the ramekins on the tray in the air-fryer basket; cook until the eggs are completely set, 15-20 minutes. Remove from basket; let stand 5 minutes before serving.

1 serving: 397 cal., 29g fat (13g sat. fat), 437mg chol., 640mg sod., 4g carb. (2g sugars, 0 fiber), 26g pro.

AIR-FRYER BACON EGG CUPS

EGGS & CHORIZO WRAPS

EGGS & CHORIZO WRAPS

My husband grew up in Southern California, and he absolutely loves chorizo. We use the spicy sausage in these wraps that our children call Daddy's Eggs.

—April Nissen, Yankton, SD

Takes: 20 min.
Makes: 6 servings

- 12 oz. fresh chorizo
- 6 large eggs
- 2 Tbsp. 2% milk
- 1 cup shredded cheddar cheese
- 6 flour tortillas (8 in.), warmed
- Optional toppings: Thinly sliced green onions, minced fresh cilantro and salsa

1. Remove the chorizo from casings. In a large cast-iron or other heavy skillet, cook chorizo over medium heat until cooked through, breaking into crumbles, 6-8 minutes. Drain and return to the pan.
2. In a small bowl, whisk eggs and milk until blended. Add egg mixture to chorizo. Cook and stir until eggs are thickened and no liquid egg remains. Stir in the cheese. Spoon ½ cup of the egg mixture across center of each tortilla. Add toppings of your choice. Fold bottom and sides of tortilla over filling and roll up.

1 wrap: 519 cal., 32g fat (12g sat. fat), 255mg chol., 1121mg sod., 28g carb. (1g sugars, 2g fiber), 27g pro.

COTTAGE CHEESE PANCAKES

COTTAGE CHEESE PANCAKES

A breakfast of cottage cheese with ketchup and pepper might seem scandalous to some, but to President Richard Nixon it was standard morning fare. The cottage cheese in these flapjacks adds nice texture and an old-fashioned flavor reminiscent of blintzes. If you want to top them with something red, I suggest strawberry syrup.

—Terri Johns, Fort Wayne, IN

Takes: 20 min.
Makes: 8 pancakes

- 4 large eggs, lightly beaten
- 1 cup 2% cottage cheese
- 6 Tbsp. butter, melted
- ½ cup all-purpose flour

1. In a small bowl, whisk the eggs, cottage cheese and butter until blended. Add flour; stir just until moistened.
2. Lightly grease a griddle; heat over medium heat. Pour batter by ¼ cupfuls onto griddle. Cook until bottoms are golden brown. Turn; cook until second side is golden brown.

2 pancakes: 326 cal., 23g fat (13g sat. fat), 234mg chol., 378mg sod., 15g carb. (3g sugars, 0 fiber), 13g pro.

OMELET WEDGES WITH CHEESE SAUCE

OMELET WEDGES WITH CHEESE SAUCE

Our kids rush to the kitchen table whenever these fluffy, layered omelets are on the menu. A savory cheese sauce tastefully tops each piece.
—Amy Transue, Catasauqua, PA

Takes: 30 min.
Makes: 6 servings

- 6 large eggs, separated
- ½ tsp. salt
- ¼ cup cornstarch
- Dash pepper
- ⅓ cup water

SAUCE

- 1 Tbsp. butter
- 1 Tbsp. cornstarch
- ¼ tsp. salt
- Dash pepper
- 1 cup whole milk
- 2 cups shredded cheddar cheese

1. In a small bowl, beat egg whites and salt until stiff peaks form. In a large bowl, beat the cornstarch, egg yolks and pepper until lemon-colored. Add the water; mix well. Fold in the egg whites.
2. Pour mixture into 2 greased 9-in. pie plates. Bake at 350° for 15 minutes or until a knife inserted in the center comes out clean.
3. Meanwhile, in a small saucepan, melt butter. Stir in cornstarch, salt and pepper until smooth. Gradually add milk. Bring to a boil; cook and stir for 2 minutes or until thickened. Reduce heat; stir in the cheese until melted.
4. To serve, cut each omelet into 6 wedges. Stack 2 wedges on each serving plate with cheese sauce drizzled both between and on top.

1 piece: 275 cal., 19g fat (12g sat. fat), 263mg chol., 624mg sod., 10g carb. (3g sugars, 0 fiber), 16g pro.

SPANISH OMELET

Wake up your taste buds with the yummy, zesty flavors of warm refried beans, salsa and shredded cheese. The best part: You can whip up this satisfying hot breakfast in 15 minutes flat. Take it up a notch with spicy salsa, or add sizzling cooked bacon for a smoky twist.

—Teresa Gunnell, Lovettsville, VA

Takes: 15 min.
Makes: 2 servings

- 6 large eggs
- ¼ cup water
- 1 cup refried beans, warmed
- ¼ cup chopped red onion
- ½ cup shredded Mexican cheese blend, divided
- ¼ cup salsa

1. Heat a 10-in. nonstick skillet coated with cooking spray over medium heat. Whisk the eggs and water. Add half egg mixture to skillet (mixture should set immediately at edges).
2. As eggs set, push cooked edges toward the center, letting the uncooked portion flow underneath. When the eggs are set, spoon half of the beans and half of the onion on 1 side and sprinkle with 2 Tbsp. cheese; fold other side over filling. Slide omelet onto a plate. Repeat. Garnish with salsa and remaining cheese.

1 omelet: 450 cal., 26g fat (10g sat. fat), 583mg chol., 944mg sod., 22g carb. (3g sugars, 5g fiber), 31g pro.

SPANISH OMELET

STRAWBERRY BREAKFAST SHORTCAKES

I don't let a busy schedule stop me from eating healthy! Protein, fruit, dairy and whole grains come together in a flash for a delectable start to the day.

—Paula Wharton, El Paso, TX

Takes: 10 min.
Makes: 2 servings

- 4 frozen low-fat multigrain waffles
- 1 cup fresh strawberries, sliced
- ½ cup plain Greek yogurt
- Maple syrup

Prepare waffles according to package directions. Divide between 2 serving plates. Top with strawberries and yogurt. Serve with syrup.

2 waffles with ½ cup strawberries and ¼ cup yogurt (calculated without syrup): 230 cal., 8g fat (4g sat. fat), 15mg chol., 466mg sod., 36g carb. (10g sugars, 4g fiber), 7g pro. **Diabetic exchanges:** 2 starch, 1 fat, ½ fruit.

BAKED EGGS WITH CHEDDAR & BACON

BAKED EGGS WITH CHEDDAR & BACON

These little treats are so easy to make and perfect for a special meal. The smoky cheese and bacon elevate eggs to a new level!
—Catherine Wilkinson, Prescott, AZ

Takes: 25 min.
Makes: 4 servings

- 4 large eggs
- 4 Tbsp. fat-free milk, divided
- 2 Tbsp. shredded smoked cheddar cheese
- 2 tsp. minced fresh parsley
- ¼ tsp. salt
- ⅛ tsp. pepper
- 2 bacon strips

1. Preheat oven to 325°. Coat four 4-oz. ramekins with cooking spray; break an egg into each dish. Spoon 1 Tbsp. milk over each egg. Combine cheese, parsley, salt and pepper; sprinkle over eggs.
2. Bake eggs, uncovered, 12-15 minutes or until whites are completely set and yolks begin to thicken but are not firm.
3. Meanwhile, in a small skillet, cook bacon over medium heat until crisp. Remove to paper towels to drain. Crumble bacon and sprinkle over eggs.

1 serving: 107 cal., 7g fat (3g sat. fat), 219mg chol., 319mg sod., 1g carb. (1g sugars, 0 fiber), 9g pro. **Diabetic exchanges:** 1 medium-fat meat.

TOMATO & GREEN PEPPER OMELET

Fresh green pepper, onion and tomato give this savory omelet garden-fresh flavors. You can easily vary it based on the fresh ingredients you have on hand.
—Agnes Ward, Stratford, ON

Takes: 20 min. • **Makes:** 1 serving

- ⅓ cup chopped green pepper
- 2 Tbsp. chopped onion
- 2 tsp. olive oil
- 1 Tbsp. butter
- 3 large eggs
- 3 Tbsp. water
- ⅛ tsp. salt
- ⅛ tsp. pepper
- ⅓ cup chopped tomato

1. In a small nonstick skillet, saute green pepper and onion in oil until tender. Remove from skillet and set aside.
2. In the same skillet, melt the butter over medium-high heat. Whisk the eggs, water, salt and pepper. Add egg mixture to skillet (mixture should set immediately at edges).
3. As eggs set, push cooked edges toward the center, letting the uncooked portion flow underneath. When the eggs are set, spoon green pepper mixture and tomato on 1 side; fold other side over filling. Slide omelet onto a plate.

1 omelet: 424 cal., 35g fat (13g sat. fat), 665mg chol., 591mg sod., 8g carb. (5g sugars, 2g fiber), 20g pro.

TOAD IN THE HOLE

TOAD IN THE HOLE

This is one of the first recipes I had my children prepare when they were learning to cook. My little ones are now grown (and have advanced to more difficult recipes), but this continues to be a standby in my home as well as theirs.
—Ruth Lechleiter, Breckenridge, MN

Takes: 15 min. • **Makes:** 1 serving

- 1 slice of bread
- 1 tsp. butter
- 1 large egg
- Salt and pepper to taste

1. Cut a 3-in. hole in the middle of the bread and discard. In a small skillet, melt the butter; place the bread in the skillet.
2. Place egg in the hole. Cook for about 2 minutes over medium heat until the bread is lightly browned. Turn and cook the other side until egg yolk is almost set. Season with salt and pepper.

1 serving:: 183 cal., 10g fat (4g sat. fat), 196mg chol., 244mg sod., 15g carb. (2g sugars, 1g fiber), 9g pro. **Diabetic exchanges:** 1 starch, 1 medium-fat meat, 1 fat.

O'BRIEN SAUSAGE SKILLET

Inspiration hit one night when I was in a time crunch. This was so satisfying and easy to make, many friends now serve it, too.
—Linda Harris, Wichita, KS

Takes: 20 min.
Makes: 6 servings

- 1 pkg. (28 oz.) frozen O'Brien potatoes
- ¼ cup plus 2 tsp. canola oil, divided
- 1 pkg. (14 oz.) smoked turkey kielbasa, sliced
- 2 medium tart apples, peeled and chopped
- 1 medium onion, chopped
- 1 cup shredded cheddar cheese

1. In a large nonstick skillet, prepare potatoes according to package directions, using ¼ cup oil. Meanwhile, in another skillet, heat remaining oil over medium-high heat. Add the kielbasa, apples and onion; cook and stir 8-10 minutes or until the onion is tender.
2. Spoon sausage mixture over potatoes; sprinkle with cheese. Cook, covered, 3-4 minutes longer or until cheese is melted.

1 serving: 377 cal., 21g fat (6g sat. fat), 61mg chol., 803mg sod., 29g carb. (8g sugars, 4g fiber), 17g pro.

O'BRIEN SAUSAGE SKILLET

ANDOUILLE SAUSAGE HASH

I threw this hash together at the last minute for a church brunch. Folks liked it so much they asked me for the recipe, so I scrambled to write it down.
—Paulette Heisler, Tampa, FL

Prep: 20 min.
Bake: 30 min. + standing
Makes: 8 servings

- 1 Tbsp. canola oil
- 1 lb. fully cooked andouille sausage links or smoked kielbasa, cut into ¼-in. slices
- 1 pkg. (28 oz.) frozen O'Brien potatoes
- 1 jar (16 oz.) cheese sauce
- 3 Tbsp. Louisiana-style hot sauce
- 2 cups shredded sharp cheddar cheese
- Thinly sliced green onions, optional

1. Preheat oven to 425°. In a large skillet, heat the oil over medium heat. Add sausage; cook and stir until sausage is browned, 6-8 minutes; remove with a slotted spoon. In same pan, add potatoes. Cover and cook over medium heat until the O'Brien potatoes are tender, 6-8 minutes, stirring occasionally. In a greased 11x7-in. baking dish, layer sausage and potatoes.
2. In a small bowl, combine cheese sauce and hot sauce; pour over potatoes. Sprinkle with cheese. Bake, uncovered, until bubbly and cheese is golden brown, 30-35 minutes. If desired, sprinkle with green onions. Let stand 10 minutes before serving.

Make-Ahead: Refrigerate unbaked hash, covered, several hours or overnight. To use, preheat oven to 425°. Remove hash from refrigerator while oven heats. Bake as directed, increasing time as necessary until golden brown. Let stand 5-10 minutes before serving.

1 serving: 443 cal., 32g fat (12g sat. fat), 126mg chol., 1357mg sod., 21g carb. (2g sugars, 2g fiber), 21g pro.

ANDOUILLE SAUSAGE HASH

EGG BASKETS BENEDICT

EGG BASKETS BENEDICT

Puff pastry turns Canadian bacon and eggs into a tasty update on eggs Benedict. We use a packaged hollandaise or cheese sauce for the finish.

—Sally Jackson, Fort Worth, TX

Takes: 30 min.
Makes: 1 dozen (1 cup sauce)

- 1 sheet frozen puff pastry, thawed
- 12 large eggs
- 6 slices Canadian bacon, finely chopped
- 1 envelope hollandaise sauce mix

1. Preheat oven to 400°. On a lightly floured surface, unfold puff pastry. Roll into a 16x12-in. rectangle; cut into twelve 4-in. squares. Place in greased muffin cups, pressing gently onto the bottoms and up sides, allowing corners to point up.
2. Break and slip an egg into center of each pastry cup; sprinkle with Canadian bacon. Bake until the pastry is golden brown, egg whites are set, and yolks begin to thicken but are not hard, 10-12 minutes. Meanwhile, prepare hollandaise sauce according to package directions.
3. Remove pastry cups to wire racks. Serve warm with hollandaise sauce.

1 pastry cup with about 1 Tbsp. sauce: 237 cal., 15g fat (6g sat. fat), 201mg chol., 355mg sod., 14g carb. (1g sugars, 2g fiber), 10g pro.

INDEX